ISBN #0-8059-4122-3
Printed in the United States of America

*First Printing*

For information or to order additional books, please write:
Dorrance Publishing Co., Inc.
643 Smithfield Street
Pittsburgh, Pennsylvania 15222
U.S.A.

# Contents

# Introduction
## *A Warning!*

**WARNING:** *The content of this book contains material that you probably have never heard or been taught in Sunday School. Only those who are willing to be challenged by what is contained in this book should proceed further. Only those who have the intestinal fortitude to consider the interesting biblical concepts contained in these pages should continue turning these pages. However, should you take the challenge to "read further," we believe that you will be provided with ample "fodder" to reconsider what you have been taught as a child. In many cases, you probably will have no opinion about the topics contained herein, because they have not—in our combined greater-than-eleven decades of living—ever been taught. Last of all, we are simply asking of you, if you continue to read, to at least press on and consider the truths that are contained in the Bible that have received little or no attention.*

While that "warning" is given with a little tongue in a little cheek, there is an element of truth behind it. Let us explain.

In *Webster's Encyclopedic Unabridged Dictionary of the English Language*, there is a little three-letter word under the *L* section. It is *lie*. Its definition is: "—*n*. **1**. a false statement made with deliberate intent to deceive; an intentional untruth; a falsehood." Although a strong case can be made that one who lies does so consciously and deliberately with the premeditation for deceiving someone, the dictionary definition also allows that the conveyor of the falsehood may be unaware that he or she is part of the continuation of the lie.

For example, before it was generally accepted that the world was not flat but round, it was asserted and taught that the earth was flat. Although there was no evil "intentional untruth" involved, those who taught such a concept were nonetheless passing on "a false statement." They intentionally—absent of evil motives—were passing on what you and I know today to be untrue. Similarly, many teachers of the concepts of the Bible have unwittingly (though some wittingly) "passed on false statements" that they themselves were once taught were true but are actually untrue, in reality a "lie." Our goal here is not to examine the motive but to preserve and pass on the truth.

While not all of the topics contained in this book fall under the category of "lie," it will become obvious to you that some *do* fall under the category. The other topics, as you will be able to judge by the chapter titles, are simply thought-provoking. This book in no way compromises the traditional, historical doctrines of salvation by the grace of God through our Lord Jesus Christ. We believe that Jesus is God and that He came to save us from sin. But along the way, there are some interesting topics Christians ought to think about.

Take for instance the chapter title, "Where in Hell Is God?" This chapter deals with what is known as the "omnipresence" of God. It asks, If God is everywhere, how can He be in Hell? Or take the chapter title, "What Happens to the Body after the Rapture?" Those Christians who have died before us went immediately to Heaven. This chapter looks at the interesting question, Where is their body until they get a "glorified" body later?

By simply reading the other chapter titles on the Contents page, we think your interest will be piqued. You may discover that you will want to read just a few of them. Or you may find yourself choosing to read the book in its entirety from start to finish. Either way, we want you to have fun with the following ideas captured on the following pages. Living the committed Christian life—to our Lord and Savior Jesus Christ—can be fun, entertaining, and intellectually stimulating. Enjoy!

# Chapter One

## *Where in Hell is God?*

Having received the warning in the Introduction to this book, let's jump right in with an idea that you have probably never been taught or considered. Just like you, we remember having been taught that God is everywhere—they call it being "omnipresent." We were taught that God is among us now. We were also taught that Jesus—who is God—is sitting at the right hand of God the Father.

At once we are confronted with an apparent contradiction: If He is among us now, how can He also be seated next to God the Father in Heaven? Naturally, the following questions arise: Does God fill the *entire* universe with His presence? Is He *really* everywhere at once? Is God, like theologians and other scholars have told us for so long, *omnipresent?* These questions naturally beg a final question: Just where *is* God anyway.

There is a story circulating in the Louisiana bayous about two young boys. The eldest was in his early teens, and his brother was just a couple of years his junior. The boys were not saints; they had been notorious for every deceptive maneuver childhood could have designed. There was not one childish prank that they had not connived against their family or their neighbors.

It was in this setting that the younger brother had attended the local church services one Sunday morning when the parish Father had been preaching about where God was. The young lad was sitting on the first row. The Father, near the conclusion of his sermon, wanted to include a teaching segment to the younger generation in the audience. So he pointed his finger by chance at the young lad and, with a stentorian voice, inquired of the lad, "Where is God?"

The young lad was caught off guard because he had not been following the sermon closely. In fact his mind had been drifting, as the thoughts of many youngsters do, toward thoughts of lunch and games afterwards. But now *he* was the center of attention. The Father was standing in the pulpit pointing toward the lad and almost shouting, "Where is God?"

Well, needless to say, the young lad had not heard the sermon preceding this event, and he was so shocked by his being singled out by the Father and being asked where God was that he never heard the last part of the sermon either. When the service was over, the lad raced home to his elder brother, who was upstairs in their living quarters preparing for their afternoon activities.

Almost breathless after his run home and his subsequent run up the stairs, the young lad told his brother that the Father thought God had been stolen and that they had done it. He followed through with that finger-pointing incident in church where the Father, almost shouting, inquired of the lad, "Where is God?" The young lad inquired of his brother if he had God. The younger brother said to his older brother, "They think *we* have God!"

That is a cute way of highlighting an important but often overlooked aspect of Christian theology. Can God become lost? Does God limit Himself to certain spatial and temporal dimensions? Is God *really* omnipresent?

Lest you think that this is mere quibbling or splitting of hairs, let us ask you this: Is God today in Hell? (If you notice, some will capitalize the word *Hell*, and some won't. There was this reported struggle between a writer and his publisher over just this issue. The writer continually capitalized words like Hell and Heaven, and when the manuscript would come back from the editor, red ink indicated that they should have lower-case letters. The writer would then reedit those corrections and send it back. Eventually the editor asked the author why he continually capitalized words like that. And the author said, "The rules of English grammar instruct that the names of persons and places should be capitalized. Heaven is a place, and so is Hell." The problem evidently arose because the editor did not believe in a literal Heaven or Hell. Obviously, we do!)

The Bible uses a few Greek and Hebrew words that have been translated into the English as "Hell." For example, the Greek word *Gehenna* is rendered "Hell" or "Hell fire" in Matthew 5:22, 29, 30, as well as in other places. *Gehenna* refers to the place in which wicked men and angels are consigned forever, separated from God for eternity. We catch a glimpse of the fate of these types of people in 2 Thessalonians 1:7-9:

> When the Lord Jesus is revealed from Heaven with His mighty angels in flaming fire, [He will] inflict vengeance upon those who do not know God and upon those who do not obey the gospel of our Lord Jesus. They shall suffer the punishment

of eternal destruction and exclusion from the presence of the Lord and from the glory of His might.

Hell is the location of the final destination of those wicked men and angels who are unrepentant. If they are confined to a place that is the *exclusion from the presence of the Lord*, they will be forever separated from God. Thus, if they are forever separated from God, then God cannot be in Hell, and if God is not in Hell, then God is not omnipresent!

This in no way limits or restricts God's power, called "omnipotence," or His all-knowing, called "omniscience." The attributes of God must still include the fact that He is all-powerful and all-knowing. But simply because He is not in Hell does not in any way decrease His deity, His power, or His knowledge and wisdom. He is still the great God of the Universe and *is* worthy of our praise, honor, and obedience. But He is not in Hell!

In the next chapter, titled, "Is God Really Everywhere?," we will look at some specific examples in the Bible that also shed light upon the myth of God being simultaneously bodily present everywhere. What is presented here in this chapter is sufficient to debunk the myth that God is bodily present everywhere at once. The next chapter merely presents scriptural references to support this conclusion. But before we move to that chapter, we want to include here a brief geography of Hell. We want to discuss an occasion when Jesus *was* in Hell, albeit temporarily. But first, let's clarify some terms.

## A Clarification of Terms

*Sheol* is the Old Testament word for Hell, and *Hades* is the New Testament word for Hell. Numbers 16:28-33 tells us that Sheol is the place the wicked dead go after life:

> Moses said, "Hereby you shall know that the LORD has sent me to do all these works, and that it has not been of my own accord. If these men die the common death of all men, or if they are visited by the fate of all men, then the LORD has not sent me. But if the LORD creates something new, and the ground opens its mouth, and swallows them up, with all that belongs to them, and they go down alive into Sheol, then you shall know that these men have despised the LORD." And as he finished speaking all these words, the ground under them split asunder; and the earth opened its mouth and swallowed them up, with their households and all the men that belonged to Korah and all their goods. So they and all that belonged to them went down alive into Sheol; and the earth closed over them, and they perished from the midst of the assembly.

But Hosea 13:9-10, 14 tells us that the righteous go to Sheol as well:

> I will destroy you, O Israel; who can help you? Where now is your king, to save you; where are all your princes, to defend you—those of whom you said, "Give me a king and princes?" Shall I ransom them from the power of Sheol? Shall I redeem them from Death? O Death, where are your plagues? O Sheol, where is your destruction? Compassion is hid from my eyes.

Sheol is a large place. It's like saying, "I'm going to Europe" to a man who wants to know specifics. He says in response, "I understand that you are going to Europe, but *where* in Europe are you going?" Ezekiel 32:18, 22-25, 29-30 tells us that there is a part of Sheol called the Pit. The Pit is a special place in Sheol for the wicked dead:

> Son of man, wall over the multitude of Egypt, and send them down, her and the daughters of majestic nations, to the nether world, to those who have gone down to the Pit. Assyria is there, and all her company, their graves round about her, all of them slain, fallen by the sword; whose graves are set in the uttermost parts of the Pit, and her company is round about her grave; all of them slain, fallen by the sword, who spread terror in the land of the living. Elam is there, and all her multitude about her grave; all of them slain, fallen by the sword, who went down uncircumcised into the nether world, who spread terror in the land of the living, and they bear their shame with those who go down to the Pit. They have made her a bed among the slain with all her multitude, their graves round about her; all of them uncircumcised, slain by the sword; for terror of them was spread in the land of the living, and they bear their shame with those who go down to the Pit; they are placed among the slain. Edom is there, her kings and all her princes, who for all their might are laid with those who are slain by the sword; they lie with the uncircumcised, with those who go down to the Pit. The princes of the north are there, all of them, and all the Sidonians, who have gone down in shame with the slain, for all the terror which they caused by their might; they lie uncircumcised with those who are slain by the sword, and bear their shame with those who go down to the Pit.

Isaiah 38:17-18 tells us that those who go to the Pit of Sheol can never escape:

Lo, it was for my welfare that I had great bitterness; but thou hast held back my life from the pit of destruction, for thou hast cast all my sins behind thy back. For Sheol cannot thank thee, death cannot praise thee; those who go down to the Pit cannot hope for thy faithfulness.

But there is another part of Sheol that is called, "The Bosom of Abraham." Jesus tells us about it in a parable in Luke 16:19-31:

There was a rich man, who was clothed in purple and fine linen and who feasted sumptuously every day. And at his gate lay a poor man named Lazarus, full of sores, who desired to be fed with what fell from the rich man's table; moreover the dogs came and licked his sores. The poor man died and was carried by the angels to Abraham's bosom. The rich man also died and was buried; and in Hades, being in torment, he lifted up his eyes, and saw Abraham far off and Lazarus in his bosom. And he called out, "Father Abraham, have mercy upon me, and send Lazarus to dip the end of his finger in water and cool my tongue; for I am in anguish in this flame." But Abraham said, "Son, remember that you in your lifetime received your good things, and Lazarus in like manner evil things; but now he is comforted here, and you are in anguish. And besides all this, between us and you a great chasm has been fixed, in order that those who would pass from here to you may not be able, and none may cross from there to us." And he said, "Then I beg you, father, to send him to my father's house, for I have five brothers, so that he may warn them, lest they also come into this place of torment." But Abraham said, "They have Moses and the prophets; let them hear them." And he said, "No, father Abraham; but if someone goes to them from the dead, they will repent." He said to him, "If they do not hear Moses and the prophets, neither will they be convinced if someone should rise from the dead."

The Bosom of Abraham is in the heart of the earth, which the Old Testament calls Sheol, which the New Testament calls Hades, and the KJV calls Hell. The Bosom of Abraham in the heart of the earth was a subsection of Sheol which is called Hell and Hades. It was that place in Hell where the righteous believers went when they died before the time of Christ.

However, this part of Hell has yet another biblical name. It is also called "Paradise." In Luke 23:43, when Jesus was on the cross, He turned to the repentant sinner and said, "Truly, I say to you, today you will be with me in Paradise." After Jesus died, Matthew 12:40 says He descended into Hell: "For as Jonah was three days and three nights in the belly of the whale, so will the Son of man be three days and three nights in the heart of the earth." But Jesus did not go into the Pit but into another part of Hell called Paradise, otherwise known in the Bible as the Bosom of Abraham. Ephesians 4:8-10 says that Jesus descended into the Paradise part of Hell to set free the righteous captives of that place whose reward for faithfulness was Heaven:

> Therefore it is said, "When He ascended on high He led a host of captives, and He gave gifts to men." (In saying, "He ascended," what does it mean but that He had also descended into the lower parts of the earth? He who descended is He who also ascended far above all the Heavens, that he might fill all things.)

After Jesus died, He was resurrected and descended into Hell to set the righteous captives free and lead them up to Heaven. Once He did this, Paradise no longer existed in Hell. In 2 Corinthians 12:2-4 we are shown that Paradise then went to Heaven:

> I know a man in Christ who fourteen years ago was caught up to the third Heaven—whether in the body or out of the body I do not know, God knows. And I know that this man was caught up into Paradise—whether in the body or out of the body I do not know, God knows—and he heard things that cannot be told, which man may not utter.

The repentant sinner could not go to Heaven with Jesus because dead people did not go to Heaven until Jesus would go to Hell to take those in Paradise up to Heaven. Today, Paradise is in Heaven. Before Jesus took Paradise up to Heaven, Paradise was a geographical subsection of Hell.

One last thing on Hell. Today paradise is no longer part of Hell. Today Hell is totally consumed as the Pit for the wicked dead awaiting the Last Judgment before the white throne of Jesus, after the one thousand-year millennium has passed. As a simple kind of picturesque portrayal of the geography of Hell, we enclose the following diagram.

**A GEOGRAPHY OF HELL**
Before Christ Descended
into Hell—Matt. 12:40

Hades (NT) =
Sheol (OT) =
Hell (KJV) =

**The Pit of Hell**
The holding tank for the
wicked dead and unjust
—Num. 16:28-33

**The Paradise of Hell**
"The Bosom of Abraham"
—Luke 16:22

**The Great Impassable Gulf**
Luke 16:26

Collectively, The Pit, Paradise, Sheol, Hades, and Hell
Are Called "The Unseen Nether Underworld"

Having shown that Jesus was at one time in the unseen nether under-world collectively called Hell (but only in the Paradise part of Hell), we believe it is clear that God is not today in Hell. Hence, we can now move on to some specific examples in the Bible that also shed light upon the myth of God being everywhere at the same time.

# Chapter Two

## *Is God Really Everywhere?*

In the last chapter, we told the story of the little Louisiana bayou boy who thought that God was somehow lost. Some of us might also have asked the question, like the little Louisiana bayou boy did, "Is God really lost?" Others of us may ask a similar question, namely, "Does anybody really know where God is?" In today's turbulent times, in which ancient belief systems that provided bedrock surfaces to stand upon have been dissolved by the acids of cynicism, these questions are good questions to ask, ponder, and answer.

Like you, no doubt, we have heard prominent theologians pontificate that God once dwelt right here among us in the here and now. Most of these prominent teachers and preachers have said that God dwelt in the here and now because they had read in Scripture that God "will never fail you nor forsake you" (Heb. 13:5). Together, these two statements yield the following conclusion: If God once dwelt among us in the here and now, and He has promised never to leave us, then God must be living right here amongst us even now. Sounds like good, sound Christian theology, doesn't it?

We have also heard preachers and teachers of the Gospel say that Jesus (Who is also God) went to sit at the right hand of His Father Who is in Heaven. Our question then is: How can He go anywhere if He is already everywhere? It has been said that Jesus went to His Father's right hand to build a residence for those who will reside there with Him throughout eternity. And when He left, He promised that He would come again and receive those unto Himself. Another question we then have is: How can

He *come* if He is always and already *here?* Obviously and evidently, something is amiss here!

As if these few things were not enough, we have also heard some of the aforementioned spokesmen (correctly) quote the Scriptures that affirm a certain condition about the time after the millennium. It is that when the New Jerusalem descends out of Heaven, there will be no need for the sun anymore because the glory of God would provide the light in New Jerusalem forever. (This is so stated in Revelation 21:23 and at first glance may not seem to fit into the discussion at hand, but it will.) Revelation 21:23 says, "And the city [New Jerusalem] has no need of sun or moon to shine upon it, for the glory of God is its light, and its lamp is the Lamb." Isaiah 30:26 says, "Moreover the light of the moon shall be as the light of the sun." After looking at Revelation 21:23 and Isaiah 30:26, we can know that the brightness of God will be *seven times* brighter than the noonday sun. If God shines like an everlasting halogen light, then it would be reasonable to assume that where God is there would be no darkness. It would seem to us that if God were radiating light brighter than the noonday sun—and if He were omnipresent—there would be no darkness anywhere! Do you sense something is amiss?

Have we been told the truth? If we have, why then does it not come clear in our understanding? Many believers are bewildered, confused, dismayed, mystified, and cannot put this all together because of all the entwined disparity embraced by eminent and "armchair" theologians who are propagating these conflicting statements. Where then can we go to find the truth about all of this? Hang on for a while longer as we peruse through the Scripture looking for the answers contained in it. For starters, let's begin in Genesis where we can read that God said, "Let us make man in our image, after our likeness: So God created man in His own image, in the image of God created He him; male and female created He them" (Gen. 1:26-27).

Those of us who are not blind from birth have eyes that give us the ability to see things around us. When we see our father, mother, and siblings, we have some general idea of the size of mankind. We do not span continents with our physical being; we are (comparatively) small. Several of us can gather in one small room for fellowship with each other. Now let's take a glimpse of the size of God. In Exodus 19:3 it says that "Moses went up unto God, and the LORD called unto him out of the mountain." And in verse nine it says, "And the LORD said unto Moses, Lo I come unto thee in a thick cloud, that the people may hear when I speak with thee, and believe thee forever." In verse eighteen it says, "And all the people saw the thunderings, and the lightnings, and the noise of the trumpet, and the mountain smoking. Verse twenty-one says, And the people stood afar off, and Moses drew near unto the thick darkness where God was."

Here is a scriptural measurement depicting God as being finite and measurable by man's standards. God is on a mountaintop; if God were omnipresent, the cloud could not hold Him. But here by His own words He clearly states His dimensions with objects with which we are all familiar (mountains and clouds). God even protects His likeness—that of being mankind-like—from His brilliance by providing a thick cloud as a barrier. The people stood afar off and observed the dark cloud hovering over the mountain. All of these objects are real and physical, and the people were able to evaluate their size with respect to the size of the universe. And there is quite a difference.

If you were to ask Moses or the Israelites, "Where is God?" what do you think they would say? Would they say that He was omnipresent? No. We suspect that they would say, "God is on that mountain. He is not everywhere."

Let's look at the Scripture where Jacob wrestled with God. Genesis 32:24-28 says,

> And Jacob was left alone; and there wrestled a man with him until the breaking of the day. And when he saw that he prevailed not against him, he touched the hollow of his thigh; and the hollow of Jacob's thigh was out of joint, as he wrestled with him. And he said, "Let me go, for the day breaketh." And he said, "I will not let thee go, except thou bless me." And he said unto him, "What is thy name?" And he said, "Jacob." And he said, "Thy name shall be called no more Jacob, but Israel for as a prince hast thou power with God and with men, and hast prevailed."

Here again we see the size of God in human terms that we can understand. God, while wrestling with Jacob, was not too much different in size from Jacob. After all, God *did* make mankind in His own image, didn't He? Back again to Moses in Exodus 33:9-11. This passage reads as follows:

> And it came to pass as Moses entered the tabernacle, the cloudy pillar descended, and stood at the door of the tabernacle and the LORD talked with Moses. And all the people saw the cloudy pillar stand at the tabernacle door: and all the people rose up and worshipped, every man in his tent door. And the LORD spake unto Moses face to face, as a man speaketh to his friend.

Think about this: God, *in* a cloud, came and *stood at the door* of the tabernacle. Therefore the cloud must have been smaller than the tabernacle, or else the people could not have recognized it as standing *at* the door. Furthermore, God was yet *smaller* than the cloud because the radiance of His brilliant glory was obscured by the cloud, His outer garment.

Yet another example of the size of God is given in Exodus 31:18. It is there that we can see the relative size of His finger. It reads, "And He gave unto Moses, when He had made an end of communing with him upon Mount Sinai, two tables of testimony, tables of stone, written with the finger of God."

Here again we can evaluate the size of God by seeing that which was written by His finger on the stone. We must not assume that He wrote with a ball point pen or even with a hammer and a chisel. When Scripture states that it was written with *the finger of God*, we must not apply our figurative assumptions as something otherwise. If Scripture had said, *by the hand of God*, it would have had a different meaning.

In Numbers 14 we read about the Israelites who God had so recently delivered from bondage in Egypt. They are murmuring against the problems associated with their newly given freedom. They were expressing their desire that God should have let them die in Egypt. They even suggested that they should die in the wilderness. Numbers 4:11-12 says,

> And the Lord said to Moses, "How long will this people despise me? And how long will they not believe in me, in spite of all the signs which I have wrought among them? I will strike them with the pestilence and disinherit them, and I will make of you a nation greater and mightier than they."

It is at this point that Moses intervened on the people's behalf:

> But Moses said to the Lord, "Then the Egyptians shall hear it, (for thou broughtest up this people in thy might from among them); and they will tell it to the inhabitants of this land: for they have heard that thou Lord are among this people, and that thou Lord are seen face to face, and that thy cloud standeth over them, and that thou goest before them, by day in pillar of a cloud, and pillar of fire by night. Now if thou shalt kill all of this people as one man, then the nations which have heard the fame of thee will speak, saying, 'Because the Lord was not able to bring his people into the land which he sear unto them, therefore he hath slain them in the wilderness.' And now I beseech thee, let the power of my Lord be great, according as thou hast spoken, saying, 'The Lord is long suffering, and of great mercy, forgiving iniquity and transgression, and by no means clearing the guilty; visiting the iniquity of the fathers upon the children unto the third and fourth generation. Pardon, I beseech thee, the iniquity of this people according to the greatness of they mercy'" (Numbers 14:13-19).

Here we see that God is fed up with the Israelites. He is even contemplating killing all of them there in the wilderness. And He would have done so had it not been for the persuasion of Moses that convinced Him not to do it. But most important of all, concerning the subject at hand (the size of God), we see yet another clear scriptural reference to the cloud which encompasses God while He accompanies His people on their journey out of Egypt. God, being in that cloud, could not be omnipresent, as the word is rightfully defined. While the Israelites,

> Journeyed from the wilderness of Sin they pitched their tents in Rephidem: and there was no water for the people to drink. Wherefore the people did chide with Moses, and said, "Give us water that we may drink." And Moses said unto them, "Why chide ye with me? Wherefore do ye tempt the Lord?" And the people thirsted there for water; and the people murmured against Moses, and said, "Wherefore is this that thou hast brought us up out of Egypt, to kill us and our children and our cattle with thirst?" And Moses cried unto the Lord, saying, "What shall I do unto this people? They be almost ready to stone me." And the Lord said unto Moses, "Go on before the people, and take with thee of the elders of Israel; and thy rod, wherewith thou smotest the river, take in thine hand and go, Behold, I will stand before thee there upon the rock, and there shall come water out of it, that the people may drink" (Exodus 1 7:2-6).

Notice the size of God here again. He said that He would *stand on the rock*. How can we read all of the literal descriptive events that describe God as a being not too much different in size than Moses and continue to think that God, in His person, spans the universe?

Before we close this chapter, let's consider one more affirmation of God's blood-relationship to mankind. We know that the creator God designed *our* bodies so that they would be different from any other species that He created. He created every species to reproduce its own kind. Men reproduce mankind, and, likewise, every other species reproduces its own likeness. We could go on at length and name a seemingly unending list of different species that God created, but we think you comprehend our interest in remaining close to the center line of thought instead of branching out and including many other species to little or no avail.

When God created different species, He created each of them with a different number of genes and chromosomes. He did this to insure that the separate species would remain separate forever. The all-omniscient creator God knew even before He laid the foundation of the Earth that some enterprising soul would try to crossbreed some of the species, and try to create a new species. As we have seen, crossbreeding does work to produce a new species, but the newly bred species is sterile and unable to reproduce its own kind. Its existence is the end of the line for that species. You can continue to produce that species by continued crossbreeding, but that species, once produced, cannot reproduce. Genesis 1:11, 12, 21 says,

> And God said, "Let the earth bring forth grass, the herb yielding seed, and the fruit tree yielding fruit after its kind, whose seed is in itself, upon the earth;" and it was so. And the earth brought forth grass, and herb yielding seed after his kind and the tree yielding fruit, whose seed was in itself, after its kind, and God saw that it was good. And God created great whales, and every living creature that moveth, which the waters brought forth abundantly, after their kind, and every winged fowl after his kind, and God saw that it was good.

We could go into the volumes of genetics already written about the many species to attempt to verify the veracity of God's Word. But if the preceding work does not convince you, reading those volumes won't either.

In the beginning God knew that He would come to Earth and become one of us. Therefore He said, "Let us make man in our image, after our likeness" (Gen. 1:26). He did come to Earth, and He did became one of us. He was born of the Virgin Mary in the city of Bethlehem. He was a man, yet He was also God. He taught us how to pray to the Father, Who is in Heaven, by saying, "Our Father, Which art in Heaven."

If God is present everywhere (omnipresent), then why didn't Jesus say, "Our Father Which art everywhere"? Has somebody been lying to us then? Have we been improperly taught? We believe so, but the teacher of this falsity has not been God. Choose you this day whom you will believe!

# Chapter Three

## *Is the Holy Spirit Everywhere?*

In the last chapter, we answered the question, Is God really everywhere? In this chapter we want to answer a similar question: Is the Holy Spirit everywhere? Whenever finite minds attempt to address infinite issues, we by necessity begin to employ non-literal words. That is one of the hazards of theology: God is infinite; man is finite. Any attempt to limit or confine God by trying to capture descriptions about God in verbal proclamations carries with it the hazard of creating in our minds distorted images and concepts of God.

For example, as we have seen in the last chapter, the concept of God being everywhere has become distorted. This was not demonstrably evil in intent. It merely represents a manifestation of trying to capture God in verbal descriptive proclamations. As theologians tried to demonstrate the greatness of God, particularly that He could move at such enormous speeds that He appeared to be everywhere at once, the language they used carried with it the adverse affect of delivering the unintended distortion that God was *literally* everywhere at the same time.

In a like manner, theologians in trying to portray the greatness and power of the Holy Spirit, also perpetrated the same adverse affect of delivering the unintended distortion that the Holy Spirit was literally everywhere at the same time. But this is not true.

So where is the Holy Spirit? And when we talk about, for instance in Acts 2:4 where it says, "they were all filled with the Holy Spirit," what does that mean? Good question. Let's look at it.

# Omnipresent vs. Omnibody

Perhaps a clarification of terms would be helpful, which we did not address in the last chapter. To say that the Holy Spirit is *omnipresent* is different than saying He is *omnibody*. To be omnipresent means that He is present at all places at the same time, but the word *omnipresent* needs a reference point. That is, when we speak of God the Father, or God the Son, or God the Holy Spirit as being omnipresent, we are referencing that statement in relationship to men, women, and children. Wherever there are God's creatures, God the Father and God the Son and God the Holy Spirit are always available to assist them, but that is different from saying that God's *body* is everywhere. To say that God's body is everywhere is to say that He is *omnibody*.

To say that the Holy Spirit is omnibody means that His body is at all places at the same time. But neither God the Father's body, nor God the Son's body, nor God the Holy Spirit's body are every place at the same time. Physically, this just can't happen. As we noted in the last chapter, let's now look at scriptural examples of the limited physical dimensions of the Holy Spirit.

## Examples of the Physical Dimensions of the Holy Spirit

In Genesis 1:2 it says, "the Spirit of God was moving over the face of the waters." He is spoken of as moving upon creation. In 2 Chronicles 20:14 it says, "the Spirit of the LORD came upon Jahaziel...in the midst of the assembly." Here the Holy Spirit enters "the midst." In Matthew 3:16 we can see that the Holy Spirit moved physically from Heaven to earth: "When Jesus was baptized, He went up immediately from the water, and behold, the Heavens were opened and He saw the Spirit of God descending like a dove, and alighting on Him." In John 14:16 we see that the Holy Spirit was to come into the world to abide with men: [Jesus said] "I will pray the Father; and He will give you another Counselor, to be with you forever." And in 1 Samuel 6:14 we see that the Holy Spirit can leave a man: "Now the Spirit of the LORD departed from Saul."

Omnipresence is different from omnibody. Omnipresence is governed by having a relationship with God. Omnipresence is governed by possessing a knowledge of God, but God's literal body does not need to be present among us for Him to be omnipresent with us.

An analogy of this is contained in the structure of the laws which govern America. When a police officer makes an arrest, say, against a gang of thieves, he is alone or perhaps acting in tandem with another officer. The force of the law does not lie in the police officers' bodily presence. The force of the law lies in the fact that if necessary, the entire national defense could be called out to physically overpower and enforce the laws duly enacted by the government. Like the presence of someone being felt by another who is thousands of miles away, so it is with the presence of the Holy Spirit among men. Paul gives us an example in 1 Corinthians 5:3a, 4: "For though absent in body I am present in spirit. When you are assembled, my spirit is present, with the power of our Lord Jesus."

In conclusion, it must be considered that words that usually have literal meaning lose that quality when speaking theologically. While the concept of God the Holy Spirit being omnipresent represents His power and authority that is always established amongst men, it does not mean that He is *physically* or *bodily* present everywhere; He is not. And to speak of Him as such is one of those "lies" that have developed as a result of the necessary hazard for speaking theologically.

# Chapter Four

## *The Divine Sperm*

In *The Mystery of the Manchild* (© 1993, Dorrance Publishing Co., Inc., Pittsburgh, PA) and *From Genesis to Maps* (© 1997, Dorrance Publishing Co., Inc. Pittsburgh, PA) we have laid out in detail the following scenario (*The Mystery of the Manchild* was written for professional clergy and academicians, while *From Genesis to Maps* was written so a sixth-grader could read it).

In the beginning, God the Father had as His "right-hand man" the Archangel Gabriel. God the Holy Spirit had as His right-hand man the Archangel Michael. And God the Word had as His right-hand man the Archangel Lucifer. (Before Jesus became God incarnate, the second member of the triune Godhead, He was called "God the Word." In Genesis 1:26 it says, "God said, 'Let us make man in our image.'" The "Let us" is a reference to God the Father, God the Holy Spirit, and what we today call God the Son. But before God became Jesus, He was not known as God the Son. Before God became Jesus, this second person of the Trinity was known as "God the Word.")

Harmony once existed throughout the universe until Lucifer rebelled. As a matter of fact, Lucifer and a third of the angels rebelled with him in attempting to raise Lucifer's throne one inch too high above God's. As a result of this, the Bible tells us that Lucifer, along with a third of the angels in Heaven, were excommunicated from Heaven. Today those angels serve under Lucifer, who became Satan, and are called demons.

Because of the fall of Lucifer and the subsequent expulsion of all those who served under him in the regal capacity executing the duties for God the Word, a void was created in the Heavenlies. God the Word was left without a body of assistants to carry out the tasks associated with being God the Word.

The first words of Genesis 1:1 say that, "In the beginning God created." The triune member of the Godhead who actually did all the creating that was created was God the Word. The Scriptures inform us that there is nothing which has been created that God the Word (Son) did not create (Ephesians 3:9; Colossians 1:16; Revelation 10:6). God the Word, Whom we today call God the Son, is the supreme authority of the Godhead. We know this because Matthew 28:18 (NRSV) says, "All authority in Heaven and on earth is given unto [Jesus]." Because God the Word possesses all the authority, His omniscience secures our future, if we would but believe on Him and put our trust in Him and obey His Word.

So, being omniscient, God knew before He laid the foundation of the earth that Lucifer was going to be cast out of the Heavenlies (and a third of the angels with him) because of his rebellion. God also knew that it would become necessary for Him to eventually replace the lot of Lucifer and his fallen angels. God the Word, Who would later become known as God the Son, needed to have a new body of replacements. God the Word needed a body. Jesus needed a new body to replace the fallen angels in ancient history. So God executed the Mystery of the Ages (Romans 16:25; Ephesians 3:3,9; Colossians 1:26) to secure a new body to serve in the regal capacity with Jesus throughout eternity. Here is His plan.

## Step One

Since a third of angels who were serving God the Word were cast out of Heaven, God created a new kind of spirit being formed in the image of Himself, in the likeness of Adam and Eve. The new spirit being was called Man.

## Step Two

God commanded Man to "be fruitful and multiply" (Genesis 1:22). From Man's reproductive efforts there would be born multitudes from which would be taken new faithful servant of God the Son to reign with Christ in eternity (Revelation 5:10).

## Step Three

God issued but a second command to Man. It was to remain faithful to Him until his last breath (Matthew 10:22, *et al.*). From the pool of offspring of Man would be selected those who endured to the end of their days in faithfulness to the Lord, obeying His Word and His commandments. Because Lucifer and his angels sinned in the midst of total blissful harmony, God wanted to insure that the new pool of Heavenly recruitments would not become faithless as did Lucifer and his angels.

In implementing His Mystery Plan, God the Word descended to earth to become part of this new creation of Man. In order for His plan to be faultless, He would have to give up His "godly" position in the Heavenlies and take on the likeness of those whom He had long ago created in His likeness. So that He could come to the earth and become a relationship-by-blood member of the human race, God the Word had to comply with His own long-ago established, unwavering precepts: God would have to become a man.

God, knowing the genealogical requirements of species reproduction, knew that the only way for Him to become truly man and to also retain his godly attributes, was for Him to become a spermatozoon. Interestingly, the Bible uses a word that is literally translated "sperm" in the Amplified version of the Bible: in 1 John 3:9 it says, "God's nature abides in us. The divine sperm remains permanently with us."

The Greek word translated "sperm" is *sperma* and means "semen." So in order to fulfill His ultimate plan, God the Word became a spermatozoon and impregnated the egg in Mary's womb. Many today believe that Jesus was implanted into the womb of the Virgin Mary as an embryo, but this could not be the case for then Jesus would not be a blood member of the human race. He would not then have any human genes to become like man. He would have become fully God with no part human. But the process of actually becoming a spermatozoon met all of the requirements of His becoming a human being and also retained for Him His godliness. He emptied Himself and temporarily gave up His kingdom to achieve this human likeness.

# Chapter Five

## *Did Christ Die for All Men?*

Perhaps another way to phrase the question-title of this chapter is: Did Jesus die for everyone's sin? Or did He die only for those who are in His body, the chosen ones? We have talked with many Christians who believe what the Bible appears to be saying that Jesus died for "the sins of the whole world" (1 John 2:2). The Bible says it. We believe it. That settles it.

Or does it?

There are two key biblical verses that have caused many to believe that Jesus died to take away even the sins of those who never confess Him as Lord and Savior. They are John 1:29, 2 Corinthians 5:14-15, and 1 John 2:2. Let's take each one separately.

### John 1:29

John 1:29 reads, "The next day [John the Baptist] saw Jesus coming toward him, and said, 'Behold, the Lamb of God, who takes away the sin of the world!'" This is obviously a generalization because the word for *sin* is singular. We know that in a world that today contains nearly six billion people, there is more than one sin. Jesus can stand in for us to pay the penalty for the sins which each of us has committed, so John's usage of the singular was meant to be a generalization.

Notice also that the generalization of John the Baptist has nothing to do with a *quantitative* statement (how much sin or how many sins there are) but a *qualitative* condition (that there is sin in the world). Another way of phrasing his pronouncement about Jesus would be to say that Jesus can take away the world's sin. The "sin of the world" is a grammatical construction that points to the location of the origin of sin: It is from the world that sin comes—1 John 2:15-16 says, "Do not love the world or the things in the world. If any one loves the world, love for the Father is not in him. For all that is in the world, the lust of the flesh and the lust of the eyes and the pride of life, is not of the Father but is of the world."

So John the Baptist is not concerned with the issue of whether or not every man, woman, and child in the universe will call upon Christ to remove his sin. John the Baptist *is* concerned with the fact that One Who *can* take away the sins confessed by mere mortals has arrived on the scene. To him this was a remarkable fulfillment of biblical prophesy.

## 2 Corinthians 5:14-15

Let's now look at the second text, 2 Corinthians 5:14-15. It reads, "For the love of Christ controls us, because we are convinced that One has died for all. Therefore all have died. And He died for all, that those who live might live no longer for themselves but for Him who for their sake died and was raised." It might be easy to make the claim that Christ died for all men, women, and children regardless of whether they confessed their sins to God, if would just eliminate one phrase in these verses: "Therefore all have died." Obviously, Paul is dealing with an issue that is different from trying to establish that Christ died to take away the sins of even those who do not repent of them.

In this passage, Paul is trying to establish that all persons have sinned. He says so in Romans 6:23: "all have sinned and fall short of the glory of God." In Romans 5: 12, he says, "As sin came into the world through one man and death through sin, so death spread to all men because all men sinned." Since all have sinned, all have died. That is why he says in the middle of Corinthians 5:14-15, "Therefore all have died." He is talking about his ministry to revive people who are dead to sin. That is why two verses later (2 Corinthians 5:17) he says, "Therefore, if any one is in Christ, he is a new creation. The old has passed away, behold, the new has come." But he is not trying to establish that Christ died even for those who reject Him.

## 1 John 2:2

Finally, let's look at 1 John 2:2, which says, "He is the expiation for our sins, and not for ours only but also for the sins of the whole world." This verse really drives us to the point of this chapter. To be an "expiation" (RSV), "propitiation" (KJV), or "atoning sacrifice" (NRSV, NIV) for sin is different from actually atoning for someone's unconfessed sin. It is much like the auto maker GM. They make automobiles "for the whole world," but not everybody drives one. Why? Because, even though they are available for anyone to purchase, not all do so.

Perhaps the best Bible translation of 1 John 2:2 is the New Century Version: "He is the way our sins are taken away, and not only our sins but the sins of all people." It is true that Jesus is "the way our sins are taken away," because there is no other way to take away the sins we have committed. Acts 4:12 emphasizes this: "There is salvation in no one else, for there is no other name under Heaven given among men by which we must be saved." But having said that, this does not mean that those who do not confess Christ as Lord and Savior and ask Him to forgive them for their sins that Jesus will go ahead by becoming the "expiation" for their sins before God. Unless we buy a GM automobile, we do not possess one. Unless we ask Christ to forgive us, unless we ask Christ to become our expiation, His death does nothing for us.

# Chapter Six

## *Does God Love Everybody?*

At the beginning of this book, in the introductory "warning," we said that we would like to present issues here that you had probably not been taught in Sunday School. We continue with that motif by asking the question, "Does God love everybody?" Let's turn immediately then to John 14:21, 23, and 16:27:

> He who has My commandments and keeps them, he it is who loves Me. And he who loves Me will be loved by My Father; and I will love him and manifest Myself to him. If a man loves Me, he will keep My Word and My Father will love him, and We will come to him and make Our home with him. The Father Himself loves you, because you have loved Me and have believed that I came from the Father.

From these few verses, we can state the following: One, God's love is conditional. Two, God loves those who know His commandments. Three, God loves those who keep His commandments. And four, God loves those who love Him. Some of you may be saying; "But I thought that God loved everybody." Perhaps we should examine that most important word, *love*, to set the record straight and set the path for this topic.

The word translated as *love* in the passage out of John is known as "agape love." Agape love is the characteristic word of Christianity. Since the Spirit of revelation has used it to express ideas previously unknown to God's children, inquiry into its usage throws little light upon its distinctive meaning in the New Testament. However, the New Testament does distinguish three separate categories of agape love:

1) In John 17:26 it is God's attitude of love toward His Son Jesus.
2) In John 14:21, 23, and 16:27, which we just quoted, it is God's attitude of love toward those who love Him.
3) In John 13:34 it is God's command to believers to love fellow believers.

Let's take a closer look at each of these three categories of agape love. Along the way, we'll look at verses that seem to be saying something that conflicts with the above three named categories of agape love.

## Agape's First and Second Categories

Before we move further, let's get a picture of the meaning behind the Greek word *agape* that is translated into the English as "love." Agape love is God highly esteeming and highly regarding someone in His creation. Now let's look at the two components of this definition. For God to highly esteem someone means that He considers that person to be a valuable prize. It means that He possesses a favorable opinion or judgment of that person. We have a negative example of this in Matthew 11:20-24:

> Jesus began to upbraid the cities where most of His mighty works had been done, because they did not repent. "Woe to you, Chorazin! Woe to you, Bethsaida! For if the mighty works done in you had been done in Tyre and Sidon, they would have repented long ago in sackcloth and ashes. But I tell you, it shall be more tolerable on the day of judgment for Tyre and Sidon than for you. And you, Capernaum, will you be exalted to Heaven? You shall be brought down to Hades. For if the mighty works done in you had been done in Sodom, it would have remained until this day. But I tell you that it shall be more tolerable on the day of judgment for the land of Sodom than for you."

After reading this text, do you think God considers unrepentant sinners as "valuable prizes" and that He "possesses a favorable opinion or judgment of them?" Of course not. He plans to exile them to a special place reserved for those who do not repent. The text used the word *Hades*, but it is more commonly referred today as Hell.

The second part of the definition of agape love means that God "highly regards" someone. "To highly regard someone" means looking upon someone and thinking about someone with affectionate feelings. When we read Matthew 3:16-17, we can easily tell who God "highly esteems" and "highly regards":

When Jesus was baptized, He went up immediately from the water, and behold, the Heavens were opened and He saw the Spirit of God descending like a dove, and alighting on Him. And lo, a voice from Heaven, saying, "This is My beloved Son, with whom I am well pleased."

God "highly esteems" and "highly regards" His Son Jesus; God agape loves His Son. And in John 14:21, 23, and 16:27—which we read earlier—it is also easy to tell who God "highly esteems" and "highly regards." It is the believers who love Him by keeping His commandments.

In our own lives, we can see the analogy. When we consider someone a valuable prize, thinking of them with affectionate feelings, do we treat them differently from those we don't prize and don't think of with affectionate feelings? Of course! So is the way with God, according to His Scripture. In James 1:12 it says, "Blessed is the man who endures trial, for when he has stood the test he will receive the crown of life which God has promised to those who love him." Do you think God's treatment of those He affectionately considers as valuable prizes is a better treatment than those He does not? According to James 1:12; John 14:21, 23, and 16:27; and other verses, yes!

Last of all, let's read John 15:10. Jesus said, "If you keep My commandments, you will abide in My love, just as I have kept My Father's commandments and abide in His love." This verse tells us that God's love is conditional—if we obey Him, He will love us. So some have asked, "Can non-Christians obey God?" And the answer to that question is, no. Just because we may do a thing or two that someone we do not know likes, it in no way renders our action love. It is but pure chance that we have done what pleases him. Besides, Hebrews. 11:16 says, "Without faith, it is impossible to please God." Non-Christians do not have faith in God that causes them to study God's Word and to do the things in it that God requires of those who love Him.

We have thus reached the conclusion that God's agape love is reserved for His Son Jesus and for those who love Him. What we will now turn to are certain Scriptures that seem contradictory to this conclusion.

## Romans 5:8

Romans 5:8 says, "God shows His love for us in that while we were yet sinners Christ died for us." According to this verse, Christ died for us; who is the "us"? Paul is writing to the Christians at the Roman church. Paul is saying that Christ died for us, the people who have become Christians. It is therefore *for Christians* that Christ died. To stress this point, we may ask the following question: If we remain unrepentant sinners, does Christ's death do anything for us or have any effect on us? No. Christ's death becomes useful only to those who repent of their sins. Unrepentant sinners can in no way benefit by Christ's death. When the end of the age comes and the Final Judgment takes place, those standing on the side that never accepted Christ as their Lord and Savior will not benefit from Christ's death. At that point, Christ's death is not for them; it is too late. They missed the boat.

Christ will have died for those who had already become repentant sinners. At the moment of our repentance, God begins loving us with affectionate feelings because He considers us valuable prizes (agape love). At the moment of our repentance, according to Romans 5:8, God expresses His love for us by allowing Christ's death to pay the penalty due for having broken God's law. Our conclusion, then, of Romans 5:8 must be that Romans 5:8 speaks of a repentant sinner's relationship with God. The subjects of Romans 5:8 are not unrepentant sinners. Therefore Romans 5:8 is not a verse that says that God loves everybody. Romans 5:8 is a verse that justifies the second usage of agape love listed above, namely, to show God's attitude of love toward believers who love Him.

## John 3:16

John 3:16 says, "God so loved the world that He gave His only Son, that whoever believes in Him should not perish but have eternal life." This is perhaps the most quoted verse used to justify that God loves everybody, including those who never repent of their sins. But because we have already established that God loves those who love Him, "the world" in John 3:16 must be Christians. From *Vine's Expository Dictionary of Biblical Words* (© 1985, Thomas Nelson Publishers), we read that the Greek definition of world allows for the "specific reference to any aggregate or general collection of particulars of any sort: used of believers only in John 1:29, 3:16-17, 6:33, 12:47; 1 Corinthians 4:9; and 2 Corinthians 5:19." To show that this is true, let's look at a few of these verses where "world" refers to "Christians."

## John 1:29

John 1:29 says, "The next day [John the Baptist] saw Jesus coming toward him, and said, 'Behold, the Lamb of God, who takes away the sin of the world!'" Did Jesus "take away" all of the sins of every person in the entire world? Not for those who remain unrepentant. When we stand in the Final Judgment as an unrepentant sinner, our sins have not been taken away. Obviously, then, John 1:29 is speaking of the sin of those who repent, not every man, woman, and child in the world.

## John 6:33

John 6:33 says, "For the bread of God is that which comes down from Heaven, and gives life to the world." Did Jesus give every man, woman, and child "life"? No, only to those who repent of their sin, namely Christians.

## 2 Corinthians 5:19

In 2 Corinthians 5:19 we read, "In Christ God was reconciling the world to Himself, not counting their trespasses against them, and entrusting to us the message of reconciliation." Did Jesus "reconcile" every man, woman, and child "to Himself"? No, only those who repent of their sin, namely Christians.

Our conclusion, then, is that John 3:16 uses the word *world* to refer to Christians. John 3:16 does not mean the unrepentant people who populate the earth. John 3:16 *is* a verse that justifies the second usage of "agape love" listed above, namely to show God's attitude of love toward believers who love him.

Now let's look at another Scripture that some have said justifies the belief that God loves everybody, including unrepentant sinners.

## Matthew 5:43-44

In Matthew 5:43-33, Jesus says: "You have heard that it was said, 'You shall love your neighbor and hate your enemy.' But I say to you, Love your enemies and pray for those who persecute you." This verse may not at first glance seem to justify that God loves unrepentant sinners. But at issue here is this: If God doesn't love unrepentant sinners, then neither should you or I. So if the "enemy" in Matthew 5:43-33 is unrepentant sinners, then we have a contradiction. So it is important to establish who the "enemy" is in this passage. James 4:4 has the answer: "Unfaithful creatures! Do you not know that friendship with the world is enmity with God? Therefore whoever wishes to be a friend of the world makes himself an enemy of God." The word *enemy* in James 4:4 is the identical Greek word as that used in Matthew 5:44. The enemy, then, is Christian believers who love the world. Again turning to *Vines Expository Dictionary of Biblical Words*, one Greek definition for *enemy* is "a professing believer who would be a friend of the world, thus making himself an enemy of God" (© 1985, Thomas Nelson Publishers). Again our conclusion must be that Matthew 5:43-46 is speaking of Christians, not non-Christians.

## 2 Corinthians 5:14-15

In 2 Corinthians 5:14-15 we read: "For the love of Christ controls us, because we are convinced that One has died for all. Therefore all have died. And He died for all, that those who live might live no longer for themselves but for Him who for their sake died and was raised." This passage does not say that God loves unrepentant sinners. It says that Christ was willing to become the death penalty due for all who would repent of their sins in order that they may receive the love of God.

## 1 Thessalonians 3:12

In 1 Thessalonians 3:12 we read: "May the Lord make you increase and abound in love to one another and to all men, as we do to you." At issue here is the issue similar to "loving the enemy" of Matthew 5:44: Are Christians to love "all men," even unrepentant sinners that God Himself does not? But in this verse, Paul is speaking of the Thessalonians' love for other Christians outside their church, in another country, namely for Paul and his missionary efforts. The "all" here refers to all Christians, even those outside their country, an important concept of agape love which is defined as "love [that] does not insist on its own way" (1 Corinthians 13:5).

## Mark 10:21

Mark 10:21 says, "Jesus looking upon him loved him, and said to him, 'You lack one thing; go, sell what you have, and give to the poor, and you will have treasure in Heaven; and come, follow Me.'" We included this verse because it presents a more interesting and illuminating light upon the time of God's not loving unrepentant sinners. The person whom Jesus loved here is the rich young ruler who was also a Jew. The question is, How could Jesus love him when he was an unrepentant sinner?

Jesus became the way of salvation after His resurrection. Before His resurrection, Jews were still considered part of the family of God. They were not counted as part of the family after they rejected Jesus as the Messiah after His resurrection. So at the moment of Jesus' engagement with the Jewish rich young ruler, the rich young ruler was still part of the privileged class of the family of God that could be loved by God. But when Jesus was resurrected from the dead, that moment became the turning point for all of mankind; membership in Heaven became absolutely tied to repenting to Jesus.

# Chapter Seven

## *What Happens to the Body After the Rapture?*

One of the foundational truths (and hopes) of the Christian Church is that Christians shall be bodily resurrected at an event known as the rapture. Although the rapture—that significant spiritual event that will make it happen—will give us "glorified bodies," they shall be made glorious starting with the same bodies we now have. At the rapture, Christian bodies will be transformed in a "twinkling of an eye":

> Lo! I tell you a mystery. We shall not all sleep, but we shall all be changed, in a moment, in the twinkling of an eye, at the last trumpet. For the trumpet will sound, and the dead will be raised imperishable, and we shall be changed (1 Corinthians 15:51-52).

Another foundational truth and hope of the Christian Church is that the rapture becomes the cataclysmic event that transports true Christian believers into Heaven. According to Scripture, we shall remain for seven years in Heaven after the rapture. At the end of that seven-year period, the Bible says we shall descend with Christ to fight with Him the infamous Battle of Armageddon.

Where, then, does the body of a person who is alive at the time of the rapture go when the rapture occurs? We know it is in Heaven, but since we shall have bodies of flesh and blood, where exactly will our flesh and blood be for seven years? Furthermore, where are the bodies of the saints who have already died as they await their transformation into glorious bodies in a twinkling of an eye at the rapture? Let's take this second question first, because it begs another question: Does the spirit and soul of a person leave his body and ascend to Heaven, leaving the body where it was when the spirit left?

Genesis 3:19 reads, "In the sweat of your face you shall eat bread till you return to the ground, for out of it you were taken; you are dust, and to dust you shall return." Psalms 104:29 reads, "When Thou takest away their breath, they die and return to their dust." At first thought, after reading these two passages, one might conclude that everyone's body will return to the dust from whence it came. But is that truly the final disposition of the body? We must not make the mistake of prejudgment without first examining all of the facts. Let's look at some additional Scriptures on this subject and then make a decision.

In the seventh and eighth chapters of Jeremiah, God, through the prophet Jeremiah, pleads with Israel to amend their ways with the result that God "will cause them to swell in this place, in the land that I gave to your father; for ever and ever" (Jeremiah 7:7). The soul of people who chose to follow other gods will ultimately be sent to Hell forever, and their bodies will return to dust, for God said, "For dust thou art, and to dust thou shalt return." But the bodies of those people who have died doing God's will shall be resurrected, and they shall be brought to the land of Israel. Ezekiel 37:13-14 reads:

> "And you shall know that I am the Lord, when I open your graves, and raise you from your graves, O My people. And I will put My Spirit within you, and you shall live, and I will place you in your own land. Then you shall know that I, the Lord, have spoken, and I have done it," says the Lord.

This passage instructs us that good, honest descendants of Adam will be resurrected from their graves, and they will live forever in the Promised Land. When Jesus was hanging on the cross at His point of death, He said, "My God, My God, why hast Thou forsaken Me?" The Bible then records that, at that moment, "the tombs also were opened, and many bodies of the saints who had fallen asleep were raised, and coming out of the tombs after his resurrection they went into the holy city and appeared to many" (Matthew 27:52-53). These bodies were the bodies of believers who had died before Jesus died. Their bodies had been placed in graves, but their souls had been imprisoned in Hades (Hell) but in a separate part of Hell called Abraham's Bosom (Luke 16:22) or Paradise (Luke 23:43). (What follows here is based upon the information presented in Chapter One. Chapter One discusses the issue of Abraham's Bosom and Paradise. If you have not already done so, it would serve you well to read that chapter before you continue here.)

Jesus, Who is the creator of everything that has ever been created, was cognizant of those who would choose to be in His body. He knew that He was going to come to earth and be born of the Virgin Mary. There He made man in His own image and likeness so that man's body would conform with His when He came. In Genesis 1:31, after He had created man, it says, "And God saw everything that He had made, and behold, it was very good." It would have been a terrible mistake for Him to make a body for man which would in any way become unacceptable later on. God simply doesn't make mistakes. He created a body for man that is everlasting.

Medical science has proven the everlasting capabilities of the body. With a self-perpetuating body like we have, the life of man was intended to be eternal—but man sinned, and that plan was foiled. However, the ones whom God "hath chosen to be in Him before the foundation of the world" (Ephesians 1:4) are the ones whose bodies will never permanently return to dust. The Body of Christ, comprised of Christians, is intended to live literally as individual bodies throughout eternity.

## The Body of Jesus

Jesus' body was never found, not in the sepulcher or any other place. That is because it will never be found; it is in Heaven, with Jesus in it, just as He planned from the beginning. Only those who are to be in His body will retain their bodies forever. In Matthew 7:13 Jesus says, "Enter by the narrow gate; for the gate is wide and the way is easy, that leads to destruction, and those who enter by it are many."

The Christian body will be cleansed unto perfection, and it will emit a Shekinah glow when he is lifted up in the air at the rapture, which marks the true point of being born again. Matthew 13:43, speaking of the Shekinah glow that will accompany Christians at the rapture says, "Then the righteous will shine like the sun in the kingdom of their Father. He who has ears, let him hear." And in Daniel 12:3 it says, "Those who are wise shall shine like the brightness of the firmament." When Jesus took Peter, James, and John up onto a high mountain, He showed them a foreshadowing of what a person's body would be like when it is in its eternal state. Matthew 17:2 reads, "And [Jesus] was transfigured before them, and His face shone like the sun, and His garments became white as light."

When Jesus left this earth, He was caught up to His Father in the same manner that those who remain alive until the last day will be "caught up" (raptured). Acts 1:9 says, "When He had said this, as they were looking on, He was lifted up, and a cloud took Him out of their sight." Jesus was raptured with His body intact; His body is now intact as He now occupies Heaven. His Word assures us that the next time His "adopted children" see Him, we will be like Him. 1 John 3:2 says, "Beloved, we are God's children now. It does not yet appear what we shall be, but we know that when He appears we shall be like Him, for we shall see Him as He is."

Christians hold the hope that the very bodies they now occupy shall be transformed in a twinkling of an eye in preparation for living eternally with that body in the presence of God in Heaven.

# Chapter Eight

## *Are Men Lesser Than Angels?*

Most of us who are older than forty or so grew up in the church under the tutelage of the historical book of all books, the King James Version of the Bible. For those of us who are older in our years, there weren't many alternatives to the KJV in the first half of the twentieth century. For four centuries the King James Version of the Bible was the standard Scripture of use. It has only been in the last few decades that we have had so many different versions of the Bible from which to choose. But for those who grew up under the KJV, most would probably remember hearing Psalm 8:4-5 quoted at one time or another:

> What is man, that Thou art mindful of him? And the son of man, that Thou visitest him? For Thou hast made him a little lower than the angels, and hast crowned him with glory and honour.

If you were not raised on the KJV, this little chapter probably won't mean much to you, but if you were, you may be interested. That is because in the New American Standard version of the Bible, the New NASB, the RSV, and the NRSV, to name just a few, those same verses substitute the word *angels* in the KJV with God. For example, in the RSV, Psalm 8:4-5 reads:

> What is man that Thou art mindful of him, and the son of man that Thou dost care for him? Yet Thou hast made him little less *than God*, and dost crown him with glory and honor.

The variation in the translation occurs because of the possibilities of translations of the Hebrew word *'elohiym*. *'Elohiym* can also mean "ruler, judge, divine one, angel, or god." *'Elohiym* is used thousands of times in the Old Testament. In the KJV Book of Psalms, *'elohiym* is translated "God" 97 percent of the time. (The Hebrew word *'elohiym* occurs 357 times in the Psalms.) In another 2.7 percent of the 357 times, *'elohiym* occurs in the Psalms (11 times, to be exact); the KJV translates *'elohiym* as the lower-case word *god*. Because *'elohiym* can also mean "ruler, judge, divine one, angel, or god," the translators of the KJV elected to translate *'elohiym* in Psalm 8:5 as "angels." In the KJV, Psalm 8:5 contains the single odd translation of *'elohiym* as "angels" throughout the 357 times it used in the Book of Psalms. Something is not quite right here. Let's look at it.

In *The Interpreter's Bible*, which contains parallel translations of the KJV and the RSV, the commentator says,

> In a few sentences the psalmist gives us his philosophy of man's place and function in creation. Man has been appointed by God to be a king, God's deputy in His world: *Thou has made him a little lower than the angels.* Another translation is "than a god." Obviously the psalmist would not say *than God* (Vol. 5, p. 50; emphasis his).

The psalmist would not say "than God" (as the RSV does) because for him—and for most of his religious contemporaries—his view of God was so great that to even mumble the truth that man was made just a little lesser than God was too much for his religious sensibilities. It was difficult for the pious man of God to place himself anywhere near the greatness of God. Similarly, the translators of what would become the world-renowned KJV Bible could also not bring themselves to put man anywhere near the camp of the greatness of God.

Another example of this kind of reverence is found in the Bible. As you are no doubt aware, the Old Testament Hebrew contains many names for God. They are: *Jehovah-jireh, Jehovah-nissi, Jehovah-shalom, Jehovah-shmmah, Jehovah-tsebaoth, Jehovah Elohe Israel, El, Elohim, Branch of Righteousness, King, Wisdom, Shepherd, Servant, Word of God,* and *Glory.* When we read the Old Testament, we will often notice that the word *Lord* is typed like this, in what is known as small capitals: LORD. Whenever we see that in our Bible, we can know that the original Hebrew word was YHWH, or, adding vowels which are not present in the Hebrew, YaHWeh (Yahweh). When the early reverent readers of Scripture came across the Hebrew word YHWH, they would not pronounce it. It was too reverent for man to speak it; it was a sacred name, so they pronounced some other sound. Every time you see LORD in your Bible, we can know that it is the name of God the early worshipers of God knew to be the most reverent name of God. Thus, they would not pronounce it because God's special name was too holy to do so. This practice continues to this day in the readings of Scripture in the Jewish synagogues.

Without a doubt, the proper translation of Psalm 8:5 is that man was made a little less than God, not a little less than the angels. The usage of "angels" is a residual act of ancient reverence that is today missing in larger contemporary Christian circles.

Aside from what is really a sociological phenomenon of not pronouncing the most sacred of names of God, there is also scriptural evidence that proves that man was made a little *less than* God. Hebrews 1:1-4 confirms the view that man was made a little lower than God:

> In many and various ways God spoke of old to our fathers by the prophets. But in these last days He has spoken to us by a Son, Whom He appointed the heir of all things, through Whom also He created the world. Jesus reflects the glory of God and bears the very stamp of His nature, upholding the universe by His word of power. When Jesus had made purification for sins, He sat down at the right hand of the Majesty on high, *having become as much superior to angels* as the name He has obtained is more excellent than theirs.

Notice the highlighted portion: Jesus **became superior to the angels**. Jesus was a man, born in the likeness of men. And according to Philippians 2:5-7, He surrendered all that was divine to become identical with man:

> Have this mind among yourselves, which is yours in Christ Jesus, Who, though He was in the form of God, did not count equality with God a thing to be grasped, but emptied Himself, taking the form of a servant, being born in the likeness of men.

Since the text out of Hebrews is talking about Jesus, it is talking about Jesus as the *human being* He became. Since as a human being—emptied of any divine advantage—He *became superior to the angels*, we must acknowledge and admit that as a human being, He is superior to the angels. And since we are also human beings, we must admit that we also became superior to the angels at our birth. And if that is so, how could the correct translation of *'elohiym* be "angels" in the KJV of Psalm 8:5?

It can't. Man was not created less than the angels. Man, being born in human flesh the way Jesus was born in human flesh, became superior to the angels at his birth. Think then of the regal importance God imparts to us as members of the ruling, reigning body of Christ who will serve as replacements for the fallen angels of Lucifer! Such a wonderful estate is reserved for those who remain faithful to Him to the end of their days (Matthew 10:22; 24:13).

# Chapter Nine

## *What Does It Mean to Be Born Again?*

In the subculture of Christianity, a number of phrases have become prominent in their usage for describing that moment when a person recognizes
his sin, his failure to live up to God's law, his need to be forgiven by God
for that transgression, and his need to pay a death penalty for that viola-
tion. It is called "accepting Christ as Savior," "coming to faith in Christ,"
"receiving Christ," "becoming a Christian, "receiving the hope of eternal
life," "gaining saving faith," "being saved," and "being born again." Certainly there are others, but these represent the most common phrases used
to determine that point in a person's life when he is no longer Hell-bound
but Heaven-bound. The interesting thing about all of these phrases is that
only two of them are (or more properly, *will be*) literal occurrences. The rest
of them are in fact non-literal metaphors or figurative statements intended
to describe the turning point from Hell-bound to Heaven-bound. In the
next chapter we will answer the question, "What Does It Mean to Be Saved?"
But in this chapter, we need to look at what it means to be "born again."

When I "accept Christ," I am not literally receiving the body of Jesus.
His body is not with us today: I cannot literally "accept Him." But I can
consciously and mentally ascend to the knowledge of the truth of Scripture that says that I must repent of my sins or be forever banished from
God's presence after the Judgment. Similarly, when I "come to faith in
Christ," I am not literally, physically moving toward the literal body of
Christ. I am simply intellectually and emotionally agreeing with God's truth
in Scripture. A similar statement can be made about "receiving Christ,"
"becoming a Christian," "receiving the hope of eternal life," and "gaining

saving faith." Each of these are true occurrences. They are just not literal events that I could record on a camera and see physical bodies moving around when it happens. But that is not the case with "being born again."

In *The Mystery of the Manchild* and *From Genesis to Maps*, we clearly lay out the scriptural evidence that Jesus is now creating for Himself a body. When Lucifer fell and was banished from Heaven along with a third of the angels who fell with him, that left God the Word Who became Jesus without a body of angelic assistants to carry out His duties associated with being the second person of the Trinity. God is now setting in motion the plan of the ages to replace that third of the heavenly hosts with new re-cruitments to serve with Jesus as part of His body in eternity. Those who become Heaven-bound become part of the body of Christ. Those who be-come Heaven-bound are now being added to the body of Christ until such time as God deems enough have been added to give Jesus the sufficient number of replacements to assist Him in His regal eternity capacities.

When God decrees that the sufficient number of converts has been added to the body of Christ, a new age will dawn; it is called the Millen-nium. But the dawn of the New Millennium is described by Scripture us-ing the metaphor of giving birth to the "Manchild" (Revelation 12:5). Scripture clearly foretells of this momentous moment (when the sufficient number of converts have been added to the body of Christ) in the meta-phor of giving birth to the Manchild. *The Mystery of the Manchild* and *From Genesis to Maps* catalog precisely the details of this event. At the appointed time, the woman who gives birth to the Manchild shall deliver into God's hands a body of replacements to serve with Jesus in eternity as replace-ments for Lucifer and his angels who were booted out of Heaven. Jesus is the "head of the body" (Colossians 1:18). Those who love Him and serve Him are His body (1 Corinthians 12:27).

The birth of the body of the Manchild takes place in five stages. The first stage is represented by the ascension of Jesus after His death. Jesus, the head of the body of the Manchild, has already been birthed. It was at His ascension; He was at that moment literally born again because He died and was raised from the dead. The next stage of the delivery of the body of Christ, called by Scripture "The Manchild," is known as the rapture of the Church. The rapture is also a momentous occurrence when those who love and serve Him will be snatched from the earth. At that moment, those who love and serve Him will "be changed," says 1 Corinthians 15:51-52:

> Lo! I tell you a mystery. We shall not all sleep, but we shall all be changed, in a moment, in the twinkling of an eye, at the last trumpet. For the trumpet will sound, and the dead will be raised imperishable, and we shall be changed.

When those who love and obey Christ are snatched from the earth in the rapture, that "change" is the literal moment when they are "born again."

They are immediately at that moment literally bodily changed and placed in Heaven. That is the literal moment of truly "being born again." Up to that "twinkling of an eye," all "being born again" means is a non-literal, metaphorical way of talking about that historic moment when we first became Heaven-bound. But the actual realization of being changed in a twinkling of an eye is yet a future event; it has not, as this is being written, occurred. The literal meaning of "being born again" is being "changed, in a moment, in the twinkling of an eye, at the last trumpet." That is one of the great hopes of Christianity; that is one of the great momentous events that awaits those who faithfully serve Christ as they live out their lives on earth.

So in closing, if we are to adhere to the literal terms of what it means to be "born again," we cannot truthfully say that we are. We do own the *hope* that we shall be born again "in a moment, in the twinkling of an eye, at the last trumpet." But we cannot truthfully say that today we have already been "changed at the last trumpet," which is what saying that we are now "born again" literally means. The last trumpet has not sounded. How could we then be literally "born again"?

# Chapter Ten

## *What Does It Mean to Be Saved?*

In the last chapter, it was mentioned how, in the subculture of Christianity, a number of phrases have become prominent in their usage in describing that moment when a person becomes Heaven-bound. The phrases most commonly used are "accepting Christ as Savior," "coming to faith in Christ," "receiving Christ," "becoming a Christian," "receiving the hope of eternal life," "gaining saving faith," "being saved," and "being born again." While there are other phrases, these represent the ones most commonly used to talk about no longer being Hell-bound.

In the last chapter, it was stated that only two of these phrases have references to literal events. The others, while definitely truthful claims, are non-literal figures of speech used to describe the turning point from Hell-boundness to Heaven-boundness. In the last chapter, we described the literalness of being born again at the rapture. It is at the rapture that Christians are added to the body of Christ which shall inherit eternal life. In this chapter, we will answer the question, What does it mean to be saved? Let's begin by acknowledging the non-literal meaning of this phrase.

"To be saved" no doubt refers to that moment when someone acknowledges Christ as Lord, thereby repenting of his sin. It is a phrase used to mark that moment when someone by faith believes that Christ died to pay their penalty of death owed for having violated God's law. When someone believes that Christ died to pay their penalty for having sinned against God, and after they have repented, then their sins are absolutely forgiven. Their sins are "washed away" (another non-literal but truthful figure of speech) by the sacrificial blood of Jesus demanded by the economy of God's law. At the moment of my repentance, I am "saved" in the sense that the snares of sin have been cut by Christ. Before Christ, the snares of sin were holding me down for destruction. Before I repented of my sins, I was in the terrifying clutches of a hideous power whose only end was to pull me to spiritual death and separation for eternity from the glorious presence of the Lord (2 Thessalonians 1:9). When I repent of my sins, Christ steps in to break the bondage of sin. In that sense, He has "saved" me from the downward spiral of spiritual death and decay. Yet "being saved" has another meaning in Scripture. Notice the future tense of each of the following verses:

Matthew 10:22: He who endures to the end will be saved.

Matthew 24:13: He who endures to the end will be saved.

John 10:9: I am the door; if any one enters by me, He will be saved, and will go in and out and find pasture.

Acts 11:14: He will declare to you a message by which you will be saved.

Acts 16:31: Believe in the Lord Jesus, and you will be saved.

Romans 10:13: Every one who calls upon the name of the Lord will be saved.

1 Corinthians 3:15: If any man's work is burned up, he will suffer loss, though he himself will be saved, but only as through fire.

These verses speak of a future "saving" or "salvation." Referring again to the future, Romans 5:9 says, "Since, therefore, we are now justified by His blood, much more shall we be saved by Him from the wrath of God." That future pouring out of wrath is that which shall come in the period of the tribulation, culminating in the infamous Battle of Armageddon, when God shall utterly destroy all who have opposed His chosen people by not repenting of their sins. "To be saved," therefore, has a futuristic element. For those of us who remain in Christ, we shall be saved from the wrath of God to be poured out upon all ungodliness and wickedness (Romans 1:18) at a period in the future known to God but which certainly shall be realized in the tribulation. In this sense, "being saved" has a very literal definition. Those who love Him and serve Him shall literally and bodily be removed from the literal wrath of God that shall be reserved for certain wicked people. At this point in the Christian's spiritual pilgrimage, since God's future wrath has not as yet been poured out, Christians are not literally "saved" from it. But we do have the hope of being saved from His wrath, as long as we remain in the safety of being "in Christ."

Since the phrases "accepting Christ as Savior," "coming to faith in Christ," "receiving Christ," "becoming a Christian," "receiving the hope of eternal life," "gaining saving faith," "being saved," and "being born again" are used as non-literal but truthful figures of speech describing that moment when we embrace being Heaven-bound, let's use another metaphor to describe what we have just said. It is a metaphor of a ship, the Ship of Salvation.

It goes like this: Jesus is the Captain of the Ship of Salvation. He is guiding His ship through the murky waters of sin. He is seeking to save those who are drowning in their own vain attempts to save themselves from having violated His Father's law. As Jesus traverses the pool of waters which is sin, He is seeking to save those who wish to be saved. When Jesus spots a sinner, He offers to him a salvo, or a lifesaver. Each drowning sinner in the Sea of Sin has the option of receiving the lifesaver from Jesus. If the sinner rejects it, he is eventually doomed to death because he cannot long wade the cold waters on his own power. But if the sinner receives the lifesaver, Jesus reels him in and places him on board the Ship of Salvation.

But wait! It doesn't stop there. The sinner is safe; that is, he is "saved" only so long as he remains on Jesus' ship, the Ship of Salvation. The sinner can, if he so chooses, jump overboard, back into the dangerous waters of the Sea of Sin. (Just as crazy as that sounds, many do choose in real life to return to sinning once Jesus has removed the stain of sin from their lives.) If the sinner "returns to his vomit" (Proverbs 26:11), he is no longer safe. He remains no longer in the protective custody of Jesus.

But if the sinner remains on board, we must acknowledge that the Ship of Salvation has a destination; it is the eternal New Jerusalem. It is Heaven. As we now speak, Captain Jesus is sailing the Sea of Sin looking for lost souls who want to be saved (rescued) from their sin. He is the only one Who can do so. Yet there will come a time when God will call His Son, Captain Jesus, home with His precious passengers. God will say, "Jesus, the time is nigh. Bring Home the Ship of Salvation. Eternal life in Heaven now awaits those who have remained in the safety of Your care."

The destination of the Ship of Salvation is the Throne of God. When it reaches port, no more may be saved by being plucked from the Sea of Sin. No more can be plucked because it is not cruising the sea. It has reached its home base; it is docked in Heaven. It will not go out again once the sufficient number of heavenly replacements has been obtained. When the Ship of Salvation reaches port and each of its passengers touches the ground of Heaven, it is then that they shall be safe for all eternity. It is then that they acquire the eternal security of forever remaining in Heaven. It is then that the phrase "once saved, always saved" has meaning. Once you and I are securely in place in Heaven, having successfully deboarded the Ship of Salvation, it is only then that we can never lose our salvation. It is only then that we cannot jump ship back into the Sea of Sin.

# Chapter Eleven

## *Shall Heaven and Earth Pass Away?*

As we have alluded to earlier in this book, we have coauthored another book titled *From Genesis to Maps*. In that book (Chapter Three), we established three things: One, civilizations existed before Adam and Eve; two, those civilizations were utterly destroyed because the sin in them had become so great; and three, when God utterly destroyed a civilization and its world, He later *renovated* it to a state of perfection to be reinhabited by human life.

We touched briefly upon the fact that the world being made in Genesis 1:3-10 is a world that is being renovated. For reference, let's read that text:

> God said, "Let there be light"; and there was light. And God saw that the light was good; and God separated the light from the darkness. God called the light Day, and the darkness he called Night. And there was evening and there was morning, one day. And God said, "Let there be a firmament in the midst of the waters, and let it separate the waters from the waters." And God made the firmament and separated the waters which were under the firmament from the waters which were above the firmament. And it was so. And God called the firmament Heaven. And there was evening and there was morning, a second day. And God said, "Let the waters under the heavens be gathered together into one place, and let the dry land appear." And it was so. God called the dry land Earth, and the waters that were gathered together he called Seas. And God saw that it was good.

In these verses the world in which we now live is being renovated out of the remains of a world destroyed before the time of Adam and Eve. The world being renovated in Genesis 1:3-10 is the world in which we now live. Our world was renovated out of the rubble of the destroyed world that existed before Genesis 1:2. Hence, the destroyed world of Genesis 1:2 became the foundation for the "radical remodeling process" of Genesis 1:3-10.

However, the process that radically remodeled the world of Genesis 1:2 is not the process of *bara*-creation found only in Genesis 1:1. (*Bara* is a special Hebrew word meaning "to create something out of nothing.") We know this because the Hebrew language uses highly illustrative and definitive words that tell us so. In the case of the world being renovated in Genesis 1:3-10, the Hebrew language never uses *bara*-create. Instead it uses other words that mean "to create out of materials already at hand." It is to create something new out of something old. The literal meaning of the process of Genesis 1:3-10 is "to recreate," but to do so out of materials already present. If I "recreate" something out of materials already in existence, I am really *renovating*.

In Genesis 1:7 we get to the heart of the matter. For reference, let's read Genesis 1:7: "God made the firmament and separated the waters which were under the firmament from the waters which were above the firmament." The Hebrew word *'asah* (aw-saw') is used here and translated as "made." This word is used thousands of times in the Bible. It refers to the simple acts of creation in which human beings engage. It means to begin with materials already at hand. It means to recreate (renovate) out of elements already present. It means to make something new out of something old.

In Genesis 1:7 God made (*'asah*) *the firmament*, the basic structure upon which the rest of the world sits. The Hebrew word *'asah* means that God renovated, remodeled, and redecorated the world of Genesis 1:2 out of the elements that were already present from the time of His *bara*-creation in Genesis 1:1. God made a new world—the world in which we live—out of an old world—the world that existed before Genesis 1:2.

We say all of this simply to set the stage for answering the question, Shall Heaven and earth pass away? We want to ask this question because there is a debate amongst those we call theologians. There is a controversy among those who take seriously the study of the things of God. It is in dispute about how long Heaven and earth will exist. Some understand Matthew 24:33-35 (quoted below), and its parallels in Mark 13:29-31 and Luke 21:31-33, to be telling us that someday Heaven and earth will no longer exist; that it will disappear altogether "into thin air" without a trace. For example, in Mr. Thomas's personal correspondence with nationally televised personality Jack Van Impe, Mr. Thomas received a complimentary book from him titled, *Everything You Always Wanted to Know About Prophecy but Didn't Know Who to Ask* (© 1980, Jack Van Impe Ministries, Revised,

Second Printing, 1993). On page 132 the following question is asked: *"Is it true that the present earth and heavens are destroyed after the Great White Throne judgment?"* Van Impe's response is as follows:

> Yes. Second Peter 3:10-11 undoubtedly pictures an explosion similar to a nuclear blast, which completely annihilates the present earth and heavens. Verse 10 states: *The heavens shall pass away with a great noise, and the elements shall melt with fervent heat, the earth also and the works that are therein shall be burned up.* In Matthew 24:35, Jesus himself said, *Heaven and earth shall pass away.* However, this transpires after His millennial reign and the Great Judgment Day have occurred.

But there are a few of us who side with the minority opinion that Heaven and earth shall always exist. Let's look at Matthew 24:33-35, spoken by our Lord Himself, as translated into two different versions of the Bible, the New Revised Standard Version (NRSV), and the New King James Version (NKJV):

| Matthew 24:33-35 | |
| --- | --- |
| **NRSV** | **NKJV** |
| "So also, when you see all these things, you know that He is near, at the very gates. Truly I tell you this generation will not pass away until all these things have taken place. Heaven and earth will pass away, but My words will by not pass away." | "So you also, when you see all these things, know that it is near; at the doors! Assuredly, I say to you, this generation will by no means pass away till all these things take place. Heaven and earth will pass away, but My words will by no means pass away." |

If we conclude that Heaven and earth are literally doomed to eventual annihilation, as some claim it is so meant in verse 35 of both versions, then what will we do with the people spoken of in verse 34 that will eventually "pass away" when "these things" are fulfilled? That is, if the generation of people which witnesses the signs of Matthew 24 contains within it Christian constituents, are we then to assume that they also will "disappear into thin air" when the "these things" are fulfilled, rather than become part of Heaven's rank?

The signs of the end of the age, alluded to in Matthew 24, are the sequentially enumerated coming events which are the "these things" of

Matthew 24:33-35. "These things" must be fulfilled during the lifetime of the generation which witnesses the signs of the end of the age. Therefore the generation which witnesses "these things" shall not pass away until the end comes—*but they shall pass away*; it will be when the "these things" have taken place. And you and I know that, for the Christian, that "passing away" is something to look forward to.

The one great and glorious thing which Christians through the ages have been waiting and praying for is "the end of the age." It is that moment when they go home to be forever with the Lord as promised in 1 Thessalonians 4:17: "Then we who are alive, who are left, shall be caught up together with them in the clouds to meet the Lord in the air; and so we shall always be with the Lord." "Come quickly, Lord Jesus" has been their prayer. It is our prayer today. Because Matthew 24 speaks of the passing away of Christians, it becomes obvious that we need to take a closer look at the meaning of "pass away" in both verses 34 and 35. Let's hop to it straightaway.

## Passing Away vs. Foreverness

In verse 34, "pass away" is referring to a generation of people. In verse 35 "pass away" is referring to three things: Heaven, earth, and God's Word. If "pass away" was meant to mean "to go out of existence," then we will have to reckon with the following passages of Scripture (although there are just four passages given below, there are many more such passages that convey the same message):

> **Genesis 13:14-15:** The LORD said to Abram, after Lot had separated from him, "Raise your eyes now, and look from the place where you are, northward and southward and eastward and westward; for all the land that you see I will give to you and to your offspring forever" (NRSV).

> **Genesis 32:13:** Remember Abraham, Isaac, and Israel, your servants, how you swore to them by your own self, saying to them, "I will multiply your descendants like the stars of Heaven, and all this land that I have promised I will give to your descendants, and they shall inherit it forever" (NRSV).

> **Exodus 31:16-17:** Therefore the Israelites shall keep the Sabbath, observing the Sabbath throughout their generations, as a perpetual covenant. It is a sign forever between Me and the people of Israel that in six days the LORD made Heaven and earth, and on the seventh day He rested, and was refreshed (NRSV).

**Leviticus 24:8:** Every Sabbath day Aaron shall set them in order before the LORD regularly as a commitment of the people of Israel as a covenant forever (NRSV).

Reading just these four passages makes it difficult even to try to think of either the people or the land as ever being annihilated. This is so especially when "to annihilate" means to become "nonexistent." What these verses tell us is that land was promised to people forever, and you and I know that in order for someone to possess something *forever* he must also live *forever*. It would be absurd (and impossible) for someone to be dead and for the survivors to say that the dead man still possesses those things, let alone to say that while dead he is going to possess it forever.

Furthermore, in these passages of Scripture, it is apparent that God has made a covenant. That covenant has been made *with people*. God apparently thinks that this covenant will last forever. If His covenant with people is to last forever, don't *people* have to last forever in order to fulfill God's Word? The question you and I must ask is, "Does God's forever and man's forever mean the same thing?" It should. If it does not, then one of us must be wrong. If God did not intend for His covenant and promise to the people of Israel to be forever, He would not say so with Scripture after Scripture that promises "foreverness." The eternality of God's covenant with His people, His land, and His Word, seems to be irrevocably permanent in Scripture. So what are we to do about what many interpret in Matthew 24 to be the annihilation of Heaven and earth?

## "Pass Away" as "Change"

If instead of the phrase *pass away* the word *changed* had been used, the conflict between being "nonexistent" and being "forever" would not have occurred. But is that an acceptable hermeneutical move? (*Hermeneutics* is simply a big word that stands for the rules of how we are to interpret God's Word.) To answer this question, let's look at a comparison study of the Greek word *parerchomia* that is translated "pass away" in Matthew 24:35. It was compiled by Dr. Finis Dake and taken from *Dake's Annotated Bible* and is used by permission.

### The Greek Word for "Pass Away"

The Greek word for pass away (parerchomia) is registered in Strong's as number 3928. This same word is translated differently in other places in Scripture. It never means annihilation. It is used in Matthew to indicate the:

1. **Passing of time** (7:28; 9:10; 11:1; 13:53; 14:15; 19:1)

2. **Events coming to pass** (24:6; Luke 21:7; John 14:29; Acts 27:9)

3. **The unchangeableness of God's Word**—Heaven and earth will be changed, but not the Word of God (Matthew 5:18; 24:34-35; Mark 13:31; Luke 16:17; 21:32-33)

4. **People passing in certain places** (Mark 6:48; Luke 18:37; Acts 16:8)

5. **Denoting neglect** (Luke 11:42; 15:29)

6. **The coming of persons** (Luke 12:37; 17:7)

7. **Never passing up duty** (Luke 15:29)

8. **Danger passing away** (Matthew 26:42)

9. **Sins passing away** (2 Corinthians 5:17118)

10. **Dying** (James 1:10)

11. **Passing away of the Heavens and the earth** (2 Peter 3:10; Revelation 21:1) or the changing of them, like old things passing away and all things becoming new at the new birth (2 Corinthians 5:17-18) in this last usage it means that they will be:

    a. **purified** by fire (2 Peter 3:7; 10-12)

    b. **delivered** from the bondage of corruption into the glorious liberty of the sons of God (Romans 8:21)

    c. **changed** to a new state (Hebrews 1:10-12)

    d. **re-created** or **renewed** to their original perfection (Hebrews 12:25-28; Isaiah 65:17; 66:22-24; I Peter 3:13; Revelation 21:1)

    e. **cleansed** of all the curse and its effect (Revelation 22:3)

From this brief study, we believe it is quite obvious that "pass away" has never meant "annihilation." Applying the word *change* to our key text, Matthew 24:34-35, it would read as follows: "Truly, I say to you, this generation will not be changed till all these things take place. Heaven and earth will be changed, but My Words will not be changed." This wording in no way adds confusion to or alters the intent of God's Word. His intent is to have generations of people permanently on earth forever and ever. Both "people" and the "earth" must endure eternally to fulfill the intentions of God as stated in Scripture. As a matter of fact, knowing that "pass away" means "change" brings to mind that powerfully transforming moment in the Christian's life when he is raptured. As we alluded to earlier, one of the great hopes of the Christian faith is when we are transformed "in a twinkling of an eye" to receive our new bodies for eternity. But remember that this passage uses the word *change*. 1 Corinthians 15:51 -53 speaks of this glorious moment:

> Lo! I tell you a mystery. We shall not all sleep, but we shall all be changed, in a moment, in the twinkling of an eye, at the last trumpet. For the trumpet will sound, and the dead will be raised imperishable, and we shall be changed. For this perishable nature must put on the imperishable, and this mortal nature must put on the immortality (RSV).

When "these things" have come to pass, *then* the Christian believer will "pass away." He will be changed in a twinkling of an eye for eternity at the moment of his rapture. Later then, Heaven and earth will also "pass away," meaning that they too will be changed. Heaven and earth will be changed by being restored to its pristine state of perfection. They will be changed in order that Christians who have also been restored to their pristine state of perfection may inhabit God's creation.

We believe it is rather strongly stated in Scripture that God's people shall exist eternally in His perfected creation that will also last an eternity. What we have left to present are minor related topics. One of them is: If people, Heaven, and earth last an eternity, what about the sun? Will it too last forever? Let's look at this:

## What About the Sun?

If people and their earth shall continue for eternity, is there any scriptural provision of celestial sunshine to light their world? Indeed there is. Genesis 8:22 says, "As long as the earth endures, seed time and harvest, cold and heat, summer and winter, day and night, shall not cease" (NRSV). Since the earth is determined by God's Word to be eternal, and since "day and night" are determined by God's Word to be unceasing, then the sun must also be eternal. This is so because it is the sun which divides the day from the night. Genesis 1:14-16 confirms this:

> And God said, "Let there be lights in the dome of the sky to separate the day from the night; and let them be for signs and for seasons and for days and years, and let them be lights in the dome of the sky to give light upon the earth." And it was so. God made the two great lights—the greater light to rule the day and the lesser light—to rule the night (NRSV).

## Summary

The best understanding of the meaning of "pass away" in Matthew 24:35 is that the world will indeed be changed, but it will not cease to exist.

It must also mean that there shall always be people living upon the earth that is eternal. And by extension, the sun must continue for eternity in order to divide the nights and days that will occur eternally over the face of the earth. Heaven and earth shall not cease to exist, but they will be changed to continue on for eternity.

Earlier we cited Mr. Thomas's personal correspondence with Jack Van Impe. We mentioned that Dr. Van Impe had sent to Mr. Thomas one of his books, *Everything You Always Wanted to Know About Prophecy but Didn't Know Who to Ask*. After receiving and reading that book, Mr. Thomas wrote Dr. Van Impe about the common misunderstanding that Heaven and earth would be destroyed. Mr. Thomas included the material we now present in this chapter. Rev. Ken Vancil, Dr. Van Impe's director of counseling at Jack Van Impe Ministries, responded to Mr. Thomas's letter with the following words:

> Dear Mr. Thomas. Thank you for your recent letter to our ministry. For many years, Dr. Van Impe believed that the earth would be destroyed at the end of the Millennium. But lately, through his study of the Word, God has brought to light some verses that state that the earth will abide forever. One of these is Ecclesiastes 1:4 which states that the earth will abide forever. Also in Hebrews 1:8 God the Father says to God the Son, "Thy throne, O God, is for ever and ever." When God says for ever, He means for ever" (personal letter to Mr. Thomas, dated February 1, 1996).

## A Look at "Perishing"

A cousin to the word *pass away* is *perishing*. If you accept that the "pass away" of Matthew 24:34-35 means "change" and not "annihilation," you may wonder about another text that uses the word *perish* in conjunction with the world. That text is 2 Peter 3:5-7. It is time to look at that word in its rightful context as well. 2 Peter 3:5-7 says,

> They deliberately ignore this fact, that by the word of God heavens existed long ago and an earth was formed out of water and by means of water, through which the world of that time was deluged with water and perished. But by the same word the present heavens and earth have been reserved for fire, being kept until the day of judgment and destruction of the godless (NRSV).

In 2 Peter 3:5-7, we read that the heavens were created first; that means that the heavens were created before the earth. It tells us that the earth was created afterwards. Our present world was formed out of water and by means of water. We also learn in 2 Peter 3 5-7 that "flooding and submerg-ing the earth with water until it perished" was God's way of cleansing and *renovating* it. After untold times of renovating the earth this way with wa-ter, God decided that,

> "Never again shall all flesh be cut off by the waters of a flood, and never again shall there be a flood to destroy the earth." God said, "This is the sign of the covenant that I make between me and you and every living creature that is with you, for all future generations: I have set My bow in the clouds, and it shall be a sign of the covenant between Me and the earth" (NRSV).

Does the fact that the earth has survived many "perishes" give any indication that the word *perish* does not mean *annihilation?* If the word *per-ish* meant absolute nonexistence, then God would have had to create a new earth every time the old one perished. This has not been the way in which God chose to perpetuate the earth; instead He renovated it. And He will renovate it only once more and that will be by fire: "But by the same word the present heavens and earth have been reserved for fire, being kept until the day of judgment and destruction of the godless" (NRSV). The fact that the earth has been cleansed previously many times (according to the Scrip-tures available to us) gives us a considerable insight into what it means by "perishing." Each time the world was cleansed, it first had to perish. If perish means annihilation, then it would be impossible to cleanse it after it perished because there would not be anything existing to cleanse. So we have to conclude that "to perish" does not mean "to annihilate." In Job 20:7, in reference to the wicked, it says, "They will perish forever like their own dung" (NRSV). As we read further in the same chapter, Job 20:12-22 depicts the state of those who have "perished forever":

> Though wickedness is sweet in their mouth, though they hide it under their tongues, though they are loath to let it go, and hold it in their mouths, yet their food is turned in their stom-achs; it is the venom of asps within them. They swallow down riches and vomit them up again; God casts them out of their bellies. They will suck the poison of asps; the tongue of a viper will kill them. They will not look on the rivers, the streams flow-ing with honey and curds. They will give back the fruit of their toil, and will not swallow it down; from the profit of their trad-ing they will get no enjoyment. For they have crushed and aban-doned the poor, they have seized a house that they did not build. They knew no quiet in their bellies; in their greed they let noth-ing escape. There was nothing left after they had eaten; there-fore their prosperity will not endure. In full sufficiency they will be in distress; all the force of misery will come upon them (NRSV).

This reading further extends the element of doubt about the permanency of the so-called state of "perish." If "to perish" means that one ceases to exist, then it seems reasonable to conclude that once one has "perished" or "passed away" and is no longer in existence, nothing more can happen to him. But that seems far from the reality of the meaning of the above passages. How can "all the force of misery come upon them" who have already "perished" if they have ceased to exist? Could "perish" mean something different than "annihilation?" Obviously it does. It is also obvious that those in Job 20:12-22 have not been annihilated. The only thing that has ceased to exist for them is the possibility of a sane and glorious life because of their rebelliousness toward God.

When God's Word says that certain people will keep on "perishing forever," this broadens our scope of the meaning of "perish" and "pass away." If God's Word is in fact unchangeable, as it so states, then the heavens and the earth must be eternal. Ecclesiastes 3:14 says that we know that "whatever God does endures forever; nothing can be added to it, nor anything taken from it; God has done this, so that all should stand in awe before Him" (NRSV). God created the heavens and the earth. This is what "God has done"; therefore, "nothing can be added to it, nor anything taken from it." God's Word is permanent; therefore, in compliance with His Word, the earth also is permanent. How do we know that God is watching over His Word? Because God says so in Jeremiah 1:12: "You have seen well, for I am watching over my word to perform it."

In order to cover the words translated from the original biblical languages into English, it now becomes helpful to define certain words generic to our discussion in this chapter. Those words are: *destroyed, dissolved, wear away,* and *rot away.*

## Destroy

*Destroy* is used 258 times in the KJV. For the purpose of this study it would be inappropriate to indulge the reader in all of these instances. It is sufficient, however, to state that this word was translated from the Hebrew word *charam,* which means "to seclude." It refers to being finally separated from God without any possibility of redemption. The phrase "utterly destroyed" is found about 50 times referring to complete destruction and cutting off of cities and nations. Let's look at three examples:

> **Exodus 22:17:** Whoever sacrifices to any god, save to the LORD only, shall be utterly destroyed.

> **Leviticus 26:4:** Yet for all that, when they are in the land of their enemies, I will not spurn them, neither will I abhor them so as to destroy them utterly and break my covenant with them; for I am the LORD their God.

51

**Number 21:2-3:** A Israel vowed a vow to the LORD, and said, "If thou wilt indeed give this people into my hand, then I will utterly destroy their cities." And theLORD hearkened to the voice of Israel and gave over the Canaanites; and they utterly destroyed them and their cities; so the name of the place was called *Hormah*.

## Destroyed and Destroyer

*Destroyed* is used 167 times; *destroyer* is used 7 times. The Greek word *Iuo* is translated as "destroy" in English. It literally means "to undo; to loosen; to release; to set free; to do away with." In 2 Peter 3:10, it is translated "melt" in the KJV: "The day of the Lord will come as a thief in the night, in the which the heavens shall pass away with a great noise, and the elements shall melt with fervent heat, the earth also and the works that are therein shall be burned up." *Luo* is translated as "dissolve" in 2 Peter 3:11-12:

> Seeing then that all these things shall be dissolved, what manner of persons ought ye to be in all holy conversation and godliness, Looking for and hasting unto the coming of the day of God, wherein the heavens being on fire shall be dissolved, and the elements shall melt with fervent heat? (KJV).

*Luo* is translated as "destroy" in John 2:19 and 1 John 3:8:

> Jesus answered and said unto them, Destroy this temple, and in three days I will raise it up (KJV).

> He that committeth sin is of the devil; for the devil sinneth from the beginning. For this purpose the Son of God was manifested, that he might destroy the works of the devil (KJV).

*Luo* was translated as "broken up" in Acts 13:43 and as "break" in Matthew 5:19; John 5:18, 7:23, and 10:35; Acts 27:41; and Ephesians 2:14. It was translated as "put off" in Acts 7:33; as "unloose" in Mark 1:7, Luke 3:16, and John 1:27; as "be loosing" in Luke 19:33; and as "loose" and "loosed" in Matthew 16:19; 18:18, 21:2; Mark 7:35, 11:2; Luke 13:15-16, 19:30-33; John 11:44; Acts 2:24, 13:25, 22:30, 24:26, Revelation 9:14-15; as "be loosed" in 1 Corinthians 7:27 and Revelation 20:3-7; and as "to loose" and "to open" in Revelation 5:2, 9.

In the twentieth chapter of Revelation *luo* means the loosing of the atmospheric heavens and the earth from the curse by fire—but not their annihilation. Of all the occasions in which *destroy* and *destroyed* are used in

Scripture, it was never intended to convey the thought of annihilation. This thought would put God's Word in conflict with itself, and that would make the Word of God unreliable.

## Wear Away

In Isaiah 34:4 (NAS), it reads: "All the host of Heaven will wear away. And the sky will be rolled up like a scroll. All their hosts will also wither away as a leaf withers from the vine, or as one withers from the fig tree."

## Rot Away

In Isaiah 34:4 (NRSV), it reads: "All the host of Heaven shall rot away, and the skies roll up like a scroll. All their host shall wither like a leaf withering on a vine, or fruit withering on a fig tree."

## Dissolved

In Isaiah 34:4 (KJV), it reads: "And all the host of Heaven shall be dissolved, and the heavens shall be rolled together as a scroll: and all their host shall fall down, as the leaf falleth off from the vine, and as a falling fig from the fig tree."

## Conclusion

As you can see, we have quoted one verse from three different versions of the Bible, the New American Standard (NAS), the New Revised Standard Version (NRSV), and the King James Version (KJV). You can also see that they are all different in that they are all translating the same Hebrew word, *charam*, differently. The original Hebrew words stand unalterable yesterday, today, and forever. The difference in the three texts comes about innocently as a result of well-meaning translators who were attempting to reveal more accurately the intended meaning of God. One has but to compile a list of Scriptures which deal with a particular subject and critique them to see if there is disagreement between them. If there is, there must have been an error in a translation, as there could not possibly have been an error in the original text because God Himself, none other than Jesus Christ, was cognizant of every "jot and tittle" in the Old Testament Scriptures, and He answered, "It is written," to many of His contemporaries when questioned.

God is the Living Word and is responsible for the written Word. Both He and His Word are infallible; only the translations are subject to error. The Word of God, in the Old Testament, has irrefutably established the eternality of the heavens and the earth. The establishment of the eternality of God's throne is assuredly proclaimed in Psalm 45:6 where it says, "Thy throne, O God is forever and ever" (KJV). And the eternality of the other elements, such as the sun, moon, and stars, is scripturally assured to endure "as long as God has a throne," as we shall now read in Psalm 72:5: "They shall fear thee as long as the sun and moon endure, through all generations" (KJV). Now let's look to see how long the Word of God proclaims that the sun shall endure.

In Psalm 72:17 we read that "His name shall endure forever: His Name shall be continued as long as the sun" (KJV). It is therefore clear from these passages of Scripture that God is intending for His people to understand that His throne and the sun are to endure forever, but how about the earth? Psalm 78:69 says, "He built His sanctuary like high palaces, like the earth which He hath established for ever" (KJV). It is clear from reading this passage that the earth is also eternal. Now let's look at a passage of Scripture that establishes the eternality of people, and then we will summarize the matter altogether. Psalm 89:3-4 says, "I have made a covenant with My chosen, I have sworn unto David My servant, Thy seed will I establish for ever, and build up thy throne to all generations" (KJV). This verse clearly demonstrates that people shall also be in existence for eternity. However, just to be sure, let's look at a few more passages.

Psalm 89:29 says, "His seed also will I make to endure for ever, and his throne as the days of Heaven" (KJV). Psalm 89:34-37 says, "My covenant will I not break, nor alter the thing that is gone out of My lips. Once have I sworn by My holiness that I will not lie unto David. His seed shall endure for ever, and his throne as the sun before Me. It shall be established for ever as the moon, and as a faithful witness in Heaven" (KJV). Psalm 104:5 says, "God laid the foundations of the earth, that it should not be removed for ever" (KJV).

Thus far we have established that the intent of God is to have the earth, the sun, the moon, and His people endure as long as He has a throne. And now for the Scripture that will shed light on the "perishing" or "passing away" of the heavens and the earth, we turn to Psalm 102:25-26: "Of old hast Thou laid the foundation of the earth: and the heavens are the work of Thy hands. They shall perish, but Thou shalt endure: yea, all of them shall wax old like a garment, as a vesture shalt Thou change them, and they shall be changed" (KJV). And Psalm 104:5 says, "God laid the foundations of the earth, that it should not be removed for ever" (KJV).

In these two passages we are told that the earth will, over the ages, accrue filth as a garment naturally does when it has been worn relentlessly without having been cleansed or changed, until it gets dirty and becomes absolutely necessary to "change" it. God's people have done this ever since God Himself gave garments to Adam and Eve, and they wore them until they needed cleansing; then they took them off, went down by the creek, washed them, and put them on again. Generation after generation lived by this lifestyle of cleansing their garments, and God, being very familiar with their pattern, thus speaking in terms which He knew His people would understand, used the term regarding the heavens and the earth: "all of them shall wax old like a garment; and as a vesture Thou shalt change them, and they shall be changed."

Referring back now to our original text (Matthew 24:33-35), we want to put its meaning in paraphrased form:

| Matthew 24:33-35 | |
|---|---|
| **NRSV** | **Paraphrased** |
| "So also, when you see all these things, you know that He is near, at the very gates. Truly I tell you this generation will not pass away until all these things have taken place. Heaven and earth will pass away, but My words will by not pass away." | "There are certain signs that must occur before I set up My Kingdom on earth. Just before I do, the end of the world will be filled with certain signs. When these signs occur, you will know that the end is near.<br><br>"There will be a generation of people which will see these signs occurring. However, they will not be changed in a twinkling of an eye until these signs occur. Their change will be at the rapture after these signs.<br><br>"After their change at the rapture, Heaven and earth will be changed. Heaven and earth will be changed by being restored to its pristine state of perfection.<br><br>"Mark My Word, all these things will come to pass exactly as I have said. My Words will never change. What I say is what I mean." |

It was never God's intention to imply that the heavens and the earth would be dropped from extinction (annihilated). In fact He has stated over and over again His intention that the earth and the heavens shall endure forever. The next time someone tells you that Heaven and earth will pass away, make sure they understand that they shall not "disappear" but become renovated by God to make them look like their pristine state before the entrance of sin into God's holy creation!

# Chapter Twelve
## *The Wife of God*

In Revelation 12:1:5, a mysterious woman is mentioned:

> A great portent appeared in Heaven, a woman clothed with the sun, with the moon under her feet, and on her head a crown of twelve stars; she was with child and she cried out in her pangs of birth, in anguish for delivery. And another portent appeared in Heaven; behold, a great red dragon, with seven heads and ten horns, and seven diadems upon his heads. His tail swept down a third of the stars of Heaven, and cast them to the earth. And the dragon stood before the woman who was about to bear a child, that he might devour her child when she brought it forth; she brought forth a manchild, one who is to rule all the nations with a rod of iron, but her child was caught up to God and to his throne.

Expositors generally agree that the woman in Revelation 12 represents the nation of Israel. There are, however, many explanations that have been offered in the just as many commentaries. But let us not so quickly agree upon this simply because conventional scholarly wisdom dictates. Let's examine the evidence firsthand to see if a justification of integrity can be found.

In the first verse of the twelfth chapter of Revelation, the woman is in Heaven. In verse two, the woman is still in Heaven but is now pregnant. Verse four depicts the dragon standing before the woman travailing in birth. By verse five, the woman has delivered The Manchild but has done so on earth. And in verse six the woman has fled into the wilderness postpartum. Obviously then, the woman cannot be a literal person. There is no known person in human history who existed pregnant in Heaven to descend subsequently to the earth beneath to deliver her child. The woman is conspicuously a symbol representative of another meaning, a literary device not uncommon in biblical literature.

Within the realm of biblical hermeneutics (the art of biblical interpretation), a symbol is a sign that suggests meaning, rather than stating it. So we may ask with curiosity, What meaning is suggested by the symbolic woman? Part of the answer lies in the crown of twelve stars upon her head. Here the usage of numbers is employed, appropriately called *biblical numerology.*

Biblical numerology is also a common literary device exploited at various places throughout Scripture. As modern-day purveyors of the book of The Revelation to St. John, we are disadvantaged in our capacity to understand adequately biblical numerology, but we are particularly afflicted in our capacity to understand the biblical symbolism used to represent the historic people of God. Our conversations are rarely sprinkled with the seasoning of a discussion surrounding the historic people of God, but the usage of symbols like the woman with a crown of twelve stars upon her head was no doubt easily understood by the author's contemporary readers. Their dialogue was intimately tied to the employment of symbolic representations. Little explanation was needed to convince John the Revelator's audience of the woman's symbolic nature. As modern-day consumers of the literature of old, a little diligent effort is required to rediscover what John intended by the symbolism of the woman.

A meager investigation discloses that the number twelve holds special significance. It is the typical number of the unbrokenness, of the irreducible completeness of the theocratic people, of the people for God's own possession. It cannot be disputed that the nation of Israel represents God's chosen people; however, Israel is far more than a people of God's own choosing. She is "the wife of God: For thy Maker is thine husband; The Lord of hosts is his name. I am married unto you" (Isaiah 54:5, Jeremiah 3:14, KJV). But the wife of God is unfaithful, a condition metaphorically portrayed in the terms of sexual reproduction. In Isaiah 26:17-18, the nation of Israel is talking to God. She says:

> Like as a woman with child that draweth near the time of her delivery, is in pain and crieth out in her pangs; so have we been in thy sight, O Lord. We have been with child, we have been in pain. We have brought forth wind (KJV).

During the prophetic reign of Isaiah, the message of God lamented the barrenness of His wife, the nation of Israel. Isaiah mourns that she has been unable to do more than "break wind." As the bride of God, Israel is expected to be fruitful and multiply, but she has not yet produced the anticipated offspring yearned for by her husband God. In spite of the words of encouragement, Israel fails to produce the child of God's longing. Read further the words of the prophet Isaiah:

> Sing, O barren one, thou that didst not bear; break forth into singing, and cry aloud, thou that didst not prevail with child; for more are the children of the desolate than the children of the married wife, saith the Lord. Enlarge the place of thy tent, and let them stretch forth the curtains of thine inhabitations: spare not, lengthen thy cords, and strengthen thy stakes; for thou shall break forth on the right hand and on the left; and thy seed shall inherit the Gentiles (Isaiah 54:1-3, KJV).

Because the nation of Israel is backslidden and unfaithful, God prophesies through Isaiah that a time would come when He would look beyond the Jewish nation to fulfill the reproductive demands of His chosen people. God's unrelenting and passionate desire to behold an offspring compels Him to employ an alternate method for obtaining the desired progeny. Isaiah 54:3 therefore prophesies the inclusion of the Gentiles into the plan of salvation for the world. The prophet Micah then declares the timetable of Israel's abandonment by God:

> But you, O Bethlehem Ephrathah, who are little to be among the clans of Judah, from you shall come forth for [God] one who is to be ruler in Israel, whose origin is from of old, from ancient days. Therefore [God] shall give them up, until the time when she who is in travail has brought forth; then the rest of [Christ's] brethren shall return to the people of Israel (Micah 5:2-3).

The "she" referred to by the prophet Micah is the pregnant bride of God. Scripture has again used the metaphor of human sexuality to portray divine intent. God is the husband; the nation of Israel is His wife. Together they conceive to bear a child. She is pregnant, awaiting their first child.

After scrutinizing Scripture, it is apparent that the nation of Israel does not produce a *single child* until the time of Revelation 12. Until "the time of the end," she will not deliver the anticipated offspring. The woman of Revelation 12 is the nation of Israel that has been destined by God to deliver His child. She represents a community of beings ordained with divine intent. When she who is now serving as the pregnant bride of God delivers the child within her womb, it will be The Manchild of Revelation 12.

So the woman of Revelation 12 is the pregnant bride of God. When she delivers, she will thus fulfill her duty as the wife of God, to produce a child out of the aching of God's own heart. Her offspring, The Manchild, will be God's long-awaited child. J.A. Seiss, commenting upon the identify of the pregnant woman in Revelation 12, remarks that,

> ...this mystic woman is in the way of motherhood. Within her body, concealed from human view but consciously to herself, there is a mystic seed, maturing for manifestation, to bring which to the birth is the one great object of His most intense anxieties.

In *From Genesis to Maps*, we have already established that Lucifer rebelled before the creation of Man. Lucifer and a third of the angels (described above in Revelation 12:1-5) were tossed out of Heaven for their sin. God set into motion a plan to replenish or repopulate Heaven with new creatures who would replace the fallen angels banished from Heaven. God's plan was simple; it was threefold.

First, He would create a new breed of spirit beings: Man. These became God's chosen people whom He intended to serve as replacements in Heaven if they proved faithful while alive on earth.

Second, God charged Man to do a very simple thing: reproduce. This command is found in Genesis 1:22: "God blessed them, saying, 'Be fruitful and multiply and fill the waters in the seas, and let birds multiply on the earth.'" Any fool can participate in this command. (Interestingly, even though some claim to be atheists, they still act in a way that fulfills God's command to be procreative.) The purpose in being "fruitful" and "multiplying" was to produce a pool of offspring whom God would select to serve as divine replacements in Heaven. The standard that would determine whether or not they would serve in Heaven in eternity is found in God's third and final step of His threefold plan to repopulate Heaven.

God's third step was to charge each person born to remain faithful to Him to the end of his days (Matthew 10:22 and others). Their reward for doing so would be to rule with Christ in eternity over a Kingdom that would last forever, hovering over an earth that would also last forever. God's wife is the nation of Israel. He wanted her to produce a special child for Him, a child who would serve with His son Jesus to assist Him in carrying out the duties associated with being God the Son, whom Lucifer abandoned because of his sin.

# Chapter Thirteen

## *Lady, You Are a Man!*

One of the truly remarkable feats of God was the creation of Adam and Eve. On the sixth day, according to the Scripture, God formed and created Man. (The body of Man was formed—out of the dust of the ground—but the soul and spirit, or the inner man, was created.) We read about this in Genesis 2:7: "The LORD God formed man of dust from the ground, and breathed into his nostrils the breath of life; and man became a living being." The Hebrew word for *dust* is *'aphar;* it means mud or rubbish. The Hebrew word for *formed* is *yatsar;* it means to mold or squeeze into shape as a potter would do with his clay. Verse seven says that the body of Man was "molded or squeezed into shape" using the "dust from the ground." The Hebrew text is highly graphic. We can easily imagine God reaching down into the ground to grab a hunk of mud or clay. As He begins to fashion it and mold it and shape it, before our eyes we see what looks like the image of Man. Is it any wonder that little children today still immensely enjoy playing in the mud?

It is also interesting what scientists have confirmed about this ancient act of forming Man from the mud and dust of the ground. Scientists have discovered that the human body contains trace quantities of every known element that exists on earth. The scientific periodic table of naturally occurring elements includes gold, silver, lead, copper, tin, antimony, iron, etc. While scientists have continued to discover more, the number of naturally occurring elements in the earth is well over one hundred. Scientists have discovered that the human body—made of the dust of the earth—contains tiny quantities of each of these naturally occurring elements.

Science has once again confirmed what we can easily know from a cursory reading of Genesis 2:7: Man was formed out of the dust of the earth. Today his body carries trace quantities of every naturally occurring element found in the ground of the earth.

One industrious soul even went so far as to calculate the market price of these elements if they could be extracted from a single human body and sold. It is about $2.30. It is an irony that Man who was crafted by God consists in a market price so low, yet we must realize that it is not the substance or dust of man that gives him value. Genesis 2:7 says God "breathed into his nostrils the breath of life; and man became a living being." Without that unique act of God, Man is nothing; he is worth $2.30. We who live in the age of opulence and plenty do not know how to evaluate nonmaterial things. We look at gold and silver and pewter and calculate its market price, yet we cannot ascertain the value of God's breathing His breath into Man. Such are the ironies of life: It is only in relationship to God that Man has any value whatsoever, even though he was formed from the rubbish-mud of the ground.

However, when it came to producing for Man a helpmate, an entirely different process was taken. From the dust of the ground every living creature was molded into shape by the hand of God. Only one creature in the world was crafted in an entirely different fashion—it was Woman. It was the *womb*-man, the man with the womb. In Genesis 2:21-22 we learn of this process:

> The LORD God caused a deep sleep to fall upon the man.
> And while he slept took one of his ribs and closed up its place
> with flesh. The rib which the LORD God had taken from the man
> he made into a woman and brought her to the man.

Some cynical women, in jest no doubt, believe that the man of today has never fully woken up from the slumber in which God placed him! Poor Man. As we shall see in just a moment, Woman was created from the best stuff of Man. She is indeed the superior gender. He stands in the shadow of her; yet God has placed him to be the spiritual head of the family, another divine irony.

Perhaps you have already heard this joke, but like all jokes, it carries an element of truth in it. Three young men were walking upon the beaches of Florida. One of them spotted a bottle buried in the sand. He took it out and began rubbing the sand and grit and dirt from it. To his surprise, a wonderfully bright and delightfully energetic genie popped out of the bottle. Enjoying the fruits of her new-found freedom, she smiled at the three men and said, "Because you have set me free from that bottle, I will grant each of you a single wish." The first immediately spoke and said, "I would like to be twice as smart as any other man." The genie simply said, "It is done."

The second, realizing a good thing, capitalized upon the first man's request. He asked to be five times smarter than any man. The genie again simply said, "It is done." "And what is that you request," the genie said to the third young man. And he said, "I would like to be ten times smarter than any man that has ever lived." The genie then said, "So be it. You are now a woman!"

So God molded and squeezed Man into shape from the rubbish-mud of the earth. And when Adam was lonely, God took from him the essence of his body and formed Woman. And Adam was no longer alone. From the following joke, we may surmise that Adam had second thoughts upon the advent of Woman in the Garden of Eden.

When Adam woke up from his slumber in which God had put him, Adam saw a creature that he had not seen before. So he said to God, "Lord God, there is another creature walking over the face of the garden."

And the Lord God said, "Yes I know, Adam. It is Eve. And I want you to like her."

"But Lord," Adam said, "she is so different from me."

"Yes I know, Adam; that is because I want you to like her," God said.

"But Lord, she is shaped so differently from me. She has bumps and curves where I do not."

"Yes I know," said God. "It is because I want you to like her."

"But Lord," Adam protested again, "she is smooth where I am coarse. And she is soft where I am rough."

"Yes I know," said God. "That is because I want you to like her!"

"But Lord," Adam protested one last time, "she is so stupid!"

And the Lord God said, "Yes I know, Adam, that's because I want her to like you!"

So out of the ground God formed Man and when He had formed Man, he caused a deep sleep to fall upon the man. God performed the first recorded miraculous surgery upon the man to form his helpmate, Eve, the woman. The first time the word *woman* appears in the Bible is in Genesis 2:22, which we quoted above. (The Hebrew word is *'ishshah*.) It is in verse 22 that we read of God making Woman out of Adam's rib. The Hebrew word *banah* is translated as "made" in verse 22. God *banah*-made Woman from Adam's rib. The Hebrew word *banah* means to skillfully form. The usual word for "made" is *'asah*. The woman being *banah*-made and not *'asah*-made carries an important distinction. It means that out of the very best of Man, Woman was made. It means that God took from the best part of Man the stuff to make Woman. It means that she is the essence of Man, but it means that she is a man of men. In Genesis 2:23 we read: "Then the man said, 'This at last is bone of my bones and flesh of my flesh. She shall be called Woman, because she was taken out of Man."

Perhaps Adam did not know it at the time, but he was making a powerful theological statement. He recognized that Woman was not formed out of the dust of the ground like all the other living creatures; he knew that she was special. He knew that her origin was spectacularly unique amongst all of creation. He knew that she was taken out of the very essence of his body; the best of what he was. So Adam said he would call her Woman, because she was taken out of Man. It is interesting that the Hebrew word translated as "dust" means mud or rubbish. Given that definition, could it be possible that the author of the following well-known nursery rhyme was a student of the Bible?

## What Are Little Boys Made Of?

What are little boys made of, made of?
What are little boys made of?
Frogs and snails,
And puppy-dog's tails,
That's what little boys are made of.

What are little girls made of?
Sugar and spice
And all things nice,
That's what little girls are made of.

When Adam gave the name Woman to the newly crafted creature who would serve as his helpmate, he was using the Hebrew word for Woman which literally means "she-man." It means "womb-man," or, more to the point, a man with a womb. Woman was formed to be a female man because she was taken out of a male man. 1 Corinthians 11:3-12 says,

> I want you to understand that the head of every man is Christ, the head of a woman is her husband, and the head of Christ is God. Any man who prays or prophesies with his head covered dishonors his head, but any woman who prays or prophesies with her head unveiled dishonors her head—it is the same as if her head were shaven. For if a woman will not veil herself, then she should cut off her hair. But if it is disgraceful for a woman to be shorn or shaven, let her wear a veil. For a man ought not to cover his head, since he is the image and glory of God; but woman is the glory of man. (For man was not made from woman, but woman from man. Neither was man created for woman, but woman for man.) That is why a woman ought to have a veil on her head, because of the angels. (Nevertheless, in the Lord woman is not independent of man nor man of woman; for as woman was made from man, so man is now born of woman. And all things are from God.)

In this text we see another irony. We have already stated that Man is the inferior sex; that Woman was crafted superior to Man. Yet God has placed Man as spiritual head over Woman. That is an irony, yet in the text above we see another irony. While Woman was formed out of Man, the propagation of the human race is for Man to be born out of the Woman. The woman, as a she-man, as a man with a womb, was formed to give birth to Man. But perhaps the more titillating irony is that Woman is literally a man with a womb. Lady, you *are* a man!